Toby Meadows is a Director of Three's Company Creative Consultancy, providing services to the fashion industry, and a Director of the womenswear label Belle & Bunty. He is a fashion business consultant and a visiting lecturer at the London College of Fashion. He writes and delivers, internationally, short courses for professional development within the fashion sector.

He also acts as a consultant to the Center for Fashion Enterprise in London, working with the next generation of talented emerging designers, helping to develop an infrastructure for their business and increase their chances of longevity.

www.tobymeadows.com

To Alice, Mae, and Darcey

First published in 2009
This revised edition published in 2012 by
Laurence King Publishing Ltd
361–373 City Road
London EC1V 1LR
United Kingdom
Tel: + 44 20 7841 6900
Fax: + 44 20 7841 6910
e-mail: enquiries@laurenceking.com
www.laurenceking.com

Additional material supplied by Giacomo J. Corrado Esq.,
James Montgomery Esq., John Richardson Esq., for Chapters
3, 4, 7, 8, and 11, and Jay Horowitz, CPA for Chapter 13.

A catalog record for this book is available
from the British Library.

ISBN-13: 978-1-85669-893-1

Designed by TwoSheds Design

Printed in Hong Kong

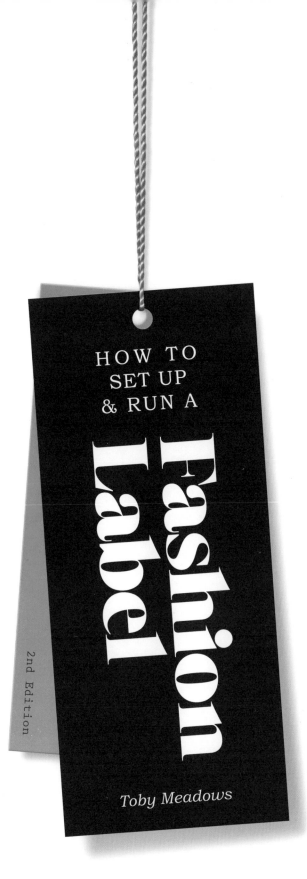

HOW TO
SET UP
& RUN A

Fashion
Label

2nd Edition

Toby Meadows

Laurence King Publishing

Contents

Author's Note

It is well documented that the world of fashion moves at an incredibly fast pace: new styles, new shapes, new colors, new designers, always the new must-haves. All of this makes the world of the budding fashion designer a very challenging and ever-changing landscape, which alone is reason enough to revise the first edition of this book. Throw into the mix a global financial crisis, a drastic increase in the cost of raw materials, a rise in the understanding of and desire for sustainable products, the growth of the social media revolution, and an explosion of interest in the world of fashion across emerging global economies, and it is easy to understand why I have returned to add to and update this book.

For this second edition I have increased and updated the section on e-commerce and included a new section on social media, consulting experts across these fields. I have expanded on the issue of sustainability and included a new case study, Christopher Raeburn, who is fast becoming the poster boy of this domain. There are four further new case studies, covering childrenswear, menswear, emerging markets, and a brand new, very talented designer, Yasmin Kianfar, who set up her label straight out of university and I am pleased to say used the first edition of this book to help her on her way. Overall I have expanded and updated the text where needed.

The global economic crisis has brought and continues to bring testing times for many fashion businesses but I firmly believe it is also a time of great opportunity. With the right product, the right distribution channels, a great understanding of your target consumer, and a little innovative thinking, anything is still possible. Continue to dream big.

Introduction: Find Your Way

Running a successful fashion label requires around 90 percent business acumen and only about 10 percent artistic ability. Most fashion start-ups are managed by the designers themselves who, while strong on the design front, may have only a very rudimentary understanding of the business of fashion, especially in the all-important formative years. As a result, although thousands of talented fashion designers and technicians graduate every year, most new fashion start-ups fail.

The aim of this book is to bridge the gap between the design and business sides of running your own label. It offers a realistic overview of the key elements needing research, development, and nurturing in the context of your own business to give your fashion label a chance to compete favorably within a demanding, unforgiving, and competitive industry. It should act as a guide through those tricky initial years and help you create a strong foundation from which your fashion label can flourish.

By working through the book, reading the case studies, and undertaking the tasks, you will gain an understanding of what your next steps should be and what challenges lie on the road ahead. This book will give you the tools to focus your ideas and ultimately help you find the right way to grow and develop your fashion business.

 Where you see this marker, you can find extra material to download free at www.laurenceking.com, including useful templates.

Sunglasses for sale in Mexico

Chapter 1: Introduction to the Fashion Industry

*U*nderstanding the fashion industry and exactly where your new label will sit is fundamental to getting your product and business right. You will need to take your time and do the research (see Chapter 7) to understand where the potential for your product will be and how buyers, journalists, and consumers will expect it to be presented to them. This chapter will introduce you to three of the key market segments: haute couture, ready-to-wear, and mass market, and will touch on the growing interest in eco fashion. It will look at the areas of fashion design and seasonality before moving on to the importance of the supply chain.

Market Segments

From the very beginning you will need to decide at which level to position your label. Many of your subsequent management decisions will be dictated by consumer expectation and will shape your business strategy. The three main market segments are haute couture, ready-to-wear, and mass market, with significant numbers of sub-levels in the latter two markets, offering a great deal of variation in product and pricing.

Haute Couture
The term "haute couture" describes luxurious, elaborately detailed and finished one-off pieces, combined with sometimes extravagant designs. Born out of the first fashion houses to set up in Paris in the late nineteenth century, couture is still at the very top end of the fashion spectrum, servicing the very few who can afford the luxurious creations that are fitted specifically to the client's every measurement. More importantly, however, for those few remaining members of the couture family, the haute couture shows in Paris represent an opportunity to showcase their design talent and act as a reminder of the immense creative ability of the designers behind the labels.

In France haute couture is a protected term, which can be officially used only by designers who meet well-defined standards set by the Chambre Syndicale de la Couture. The terms "bespoke" and "made-to-measure" may also be used for any garment that is created for a specific client, but are quite often found in the realms of menswear. To add to the confusion, many designers say their work is haute couture when, technically, it is not, and made-to-measure can also describe a service whereby ready-to-wear garments are adjusted to fit the specific needs of the customer.

Bora Aksu Fall/Winter 2011 at London Fashion Week

Ready-To-Wear

Ready-to-wear, otherwise known as prêt-à-porter, became a viable alternative to haute couture in the 1960s when fashion houses started to showcase designs that came in a range of standard sizes that could be bought directly from boutiques. By doing away with the necessity of long fitting sessions, ready-to-wear was far less expensive and therefore instantly more accessible to a wider audience. Most of the designer fashion bought today is considered ready-to-wear. Whereas couture is still shown twice a year in Paris, ready-to-wear is showcased all around the world at a number of different fashion weeks, principally in New York, London, Paris, and Milan. Today, ready-to-wear is a cross between haute couture and the mass market. Although not made for the individual, great care and detail is taken in the design and finishing, and the numbers of each garment produced tend to be low, thereby making them exclusive and expensive.

The larger, high-end designer ready-to-wear labels also develop diffusion ranges to sell at a low to mid price point. Examples of this are Marc by Marc Jacobs and See by Chloé. By creating a separate label, designers are able to tap into a much larger consumer base while protecting the aspirational brand identity they have created for their main line.

Ready-to-wear labels often wholesale their collections to boutiques and department stores by showcasing at the fashion weeks held seasonally twice a year. Typically they work 12 months in advance, researching and developing their collection for the trade fairs at which they will sell, then going into production when they have taken forward orders from the boutiques and department stores. This allows them to produce only the number of garments ordered, thereby minimizing the risk of overproduction as well as the initial expense in outlay to their manufacturer. Many designers also open their own retail outlets, allowing them to give their complete offer directly to the consumer and maximizing their margins by cutting out the middleman.

Show Calendar (Northern Hemisphere)

Month	Show	Season
January	Couture (Paris)	Spring/summer
February/March	Ready-to-wear—all	Fall/winter
July	Couture (Paris)	Fall/winter
September/October	Ready-to-wear—all	Spring/summer

Examples of internationally renowned ready-to-wear labels include Chloé, Gucci, Ralph Lauren, and Burberry. However, ready-to-wear is now an extremely diverse market with a number of sub-levels, including luxury, high-end, mid-level, and premium design. Each level will distinguish brands by product offer, price points, marketing strategies, and distribution outlets.

Mass Market

Today most people wear mass market fashion, which caters for an even wider range of customers than ready-to-wear. Clothes are produced in very large quantities and in a good range of standard sizing, making them less expensive and more accessible to the average consumer. Designers often adapt the trends set by the big names in fashion at the high end of the market. By being creative with cheaper materials and production techniques, and by working hard to stay within their customers' taste levels, they are able to produce affordable fashion. However, mass market designers cannot rely solely on inspiration from the leading catwalk designers, and are always looking at other areas for trend inspiration.

Mass market fashion is produced first and then sold through retail distribution outlets, typically owned by the brand (Topshop, H&M, Zara, Gap, and so on). A large element of risk is involved, as it is difficult to predict exactly what product will be sold. However, by designing, manufacturing, and then selling the product at retail prices, the brand will make the biggest profit margins available while offering flexibility in pricing to maintain competitiveness.

Your product line will fit somewhere within these three broad markets. Working out which market and researching it thoroughly is your starting point. Your research will identify a number of smaller sub-markets and even niche markets within each. One such market, developing rapidly and breaking into bigger mainstream markets, is eco fashion.

Eco Fashion

There is now an industry-wide awareness of sustainable sourcing and ethical employment and production practices. This has led to a growth in consultancies that specialize in helping fashion businesses develop their sustainable practices. One such specialist, Ei8ht, works with businesses, universities, government agencies, and industry stakeholders to provide training, develop sustainable sourcing strategies, create trade development programs, and project manage innovative product initiatives that address supply chain challenges. The aim of Ei8ht's work is to focus on maximizing positive impact and reducing negative impact, working with businesses to create customer-facing initiatives that have a story to tell.

The emergence of exhibitions like Estethica at London Fashion Week shows the growing importance of the eco and ethical fashion movement

Interview with Claire Hamer, Founder of Ei8ht

www.ei8ht.org

How do you define sustainable fashion?

Sustainable fashion to me is about fashion that maximizes positive impacts and minimizes negative impacts on the people and environment where it is sourced. I do not believe we need to grow the sustainable fashion industry—we need to make the fashion industry more sustainable. Sustainability means so many different things to different people that we need to find engaging positive stories that ultimately will help the fashion industry become more sustainable.

How has the fashion industry's attitude to sustainable practices changed over the past ten years?

Ten years ago, although this is when many CSR (Corporate Social Responsibility) departments were first established, many in the sourcing departments were not taking sustainable practices seriously. We are incredibly lucky that as the issues have become more prominent and an entire new area of the industry has developed so have technology and social media. This means that we now have the power as consumers to spread stories more quickly, and this has enabled the fashion industry to tap into the exciting and inspiring stories that surround fashion that is sourced with people and the planet in mind. Although the recession has in some ways made it harder for "sustainable fashion" brands to compete, it has also created an opportunity for the larger brands and retailers to really analyze why people buy into their collections, and they have begun to understand that by focusing on the stories behind the products you can really add value and brand loyalty to a business. We see more and more choice on the market due to a developing variety of fabrics and consumers' renewed interest in craftsmanship and heritage. This means that there is more for the media to talk about and this in turn has made the fashion industry's attitude to sustainable practices much more positive.

How have the customers' views changed?

Again, in social media we now have a platform for consumers to make their values known. I believe consumers are definitely more engaged in knowing how their products are made and by whom; they just don't have enough choice yet. There will always be those who simply buy at the lowest price, but for an industry to change direction it does not need every single customer to change their view—just enough of them!

Why do you think new labels should consider sustainability when starting their businesses?

There is so much competition in the market today, a story will certainly help a brand but they must make sure they consider the product first. The story must be positive, so coverage of sustainable practices would be an advantage. There are so many ways a brand can engage in sustainability e.g. local production, working with small workshops that follow fair trade principles, looking at using more eco-friendly fabrics or craftsmanship. Also, any brand starting today would be foolish not to engage in sustainability in some form from the outset, as this is the direction the industry is heading. As a new, exciting, and innovative brand they should be one step ahead of the game. Eventually, sustainable business models in fashion will need to follow a quadruple bottom line—product, people,

Designer Nin Castle, founder of award-winning label Goodone, uses recycled materials in her clothes

planet, and profit. With the challenges we face, such as water shortages, there will come a point when a collection made with sustainability in mind will be cheaper than one that is produced unsustainably. Government policy and taxation will heavily affect the costs of our sourcing decisions.

Product Areas of Fashion Design

While the fashion industry offers a broad spectrum of product categories from which you can choose to start your business, you would be wise to start by focusing on just one area. The more specific the market you target, the greater the chance of developing a strong message for your label and delivering a great product to your buyers, press, and consumers alike.

Different product categories may also have different selling seasons—which means different buyers and press to attract and more manufacturers to oversee, all of which takes a great deal of time, energy, and money to do well. Once your label has established a strong base you may well then look to increase your product range, but consider areas that will complement your existing offer. If you are selling women's eveningwear, complementary products may include shoes, bags, jewelry, and perfume. The chart below shows the typical areas that many new fashion start-ups choose to specialize in.

Product Areas for Fashion Design

Area	Brief	Market
Women's daywear	Practical, comfortable, fashionable	Haute couture, ready-to-wear, mass market
Women's eveningwear	Glamorous, sophisticated, right for the occasion	Haute couture, ready-to-wear, mass market
Women's lingerie	Glamorous, comfortable, washable	Haute couture, ready-to-wear, mass market
Men's daywear	Casual, practical, comfortable	Tailoring, ready-to-wear, mass market
Men's eveningwear	Smart, elegant, formal, right for the occasion	Tailoring, ready-to-wear, mass market
Boys' wear	Practical, hard-wearing, washable, inexpensive	Ready-to-wear, mass market
Girls' wear	Pretty, colorful, practical, washable, inexpensive	Ready-to-wear, mass market
Teenage wear	Highly fashion-conscious, comfortable, inexpensive	Ready-to-wear, mass market
Sportswear	Comfortable, practical, well-ventilated, washable	Ready-to-wear, mass market
Knitwear	Right weight and color for the season	Ready-to-wear, mass market
Outerwear	Stylish, warm, right weight and color for the season	Ready-to-wear, mass market
Bridalwear	Sumptuous, glamorous, classic	Haute couture, ready-to-wear, mass market
Accessories	Striking, fashionable	Haute couture, ready-to-wear, mass market

Source: *The Fashion Handbook*

Fashion labels Schumacher and Karen Walker (see pages 98 and 152) started off with just a few key pieces and have grown very cleverly from there. Buyers and consumers will always look for quality over quantity, so focus and refine your offer as much as possible when starting out.

Chain retailers like Burton adapt trends taken from high-end designers and mass produce them

*Designer Karen Walker,
despite starting off with
clothing alone, has branched
into sunglasses and jewelry
among other products*

Seasonality

Traditionally a fashion season is defined by weather patterns, with designers typically working to two seasons a year—fall/winter and spring/summer. By separating these seasons, the key fabrics, colors, and shapes can be determined by climate. It is quite typical for established designers to introduce a high summer range as well as a holiday season collection, increasing the number of seasons to four.

In retail management, however, a season may be looked at more from a financial perspective. A retail manager will identify a season in terms of a period of time during which the product is sold at full price, at a reduced price, and at clearance price. Determining a product's shelf-life is important. If demand continues, stock will need to be replenished, while stock that is not selling will have to be promoted to clear.

Typical Designer Trading Year (Northern Hemisphere)

Season	Calendar
Fall/winter	August to January
Holiday range (optional)	November
Spring/summer	January to July
High summer (optional)	May/June

Typical Fast Fashion Trading Year (Northern Hemisphere)

Season	Calendar
Early spring	January/February
Spring	February/March
Early summer	April/May
Summer sale	June
High summer	July
Transitional fall	July/August
Fall	September/October
Party wear	November
Christmas/transitional spring	December
Winter sale	December/January

The mid 1990s saw a revolution in the way major chain retailers deliver fashion seasons to the consumer. The "fast fashion" movement has meant a move away from the traditional two seasons a year in favor of shorter seasons taking place more frequently. Fast fashion allows major retailers, such as H&M, Zara, and Topshop, to offer new ranges every few weeks. It also allows them

1. BUSINESS STRATEGY

2. MARKET RESEARCH

3. DESIGN DEVELOPMENT

to follow trends more closely by adapting very quickly to market changes and, more importantly, to control their stock levels more efficiently.

It is still too early to determine exactly how the fast fashion movement will affect the higher end of the fashion market but it has certainly changed how many consumers are buying their fashion. Many designers and high-end retailers have begun to place a great deal of importance on pre-collections, introducing products a couple of months before the major catwalk shows take place (see Chapter 11). Fast fashion has also raised the expectation of value for money, as many chain retailers are able to offer trend-driven product at very cheap prices with an ever-improving standard of quality.

The key to success in delivering to these new fast fashion seasonal timelines is your supply chain. The better and faster your supply chain, the more flexibility your business will have and the greater the opportunity to offer more collections in a year. Even if, like most small labels, you will be working to a two-season-a-year sales strategy, your supply chain will be of the highest importance to your success.

The Supply Chain

"Supply chain" is the term used to describe the process of planning, implementing, and controlling the flow and storage of your products, from their point of origin to their point of consumption, in order to meet your customers' needs. It has taken on more importance with the current trend for offshore production and fast fashion, and is very closely monitored by big chain retailers. You must manage your supply chain effectively if you are to maximize profit margins and minimize wastage. Supply chains can seem very complicated, but the illustration on these pages shows a basic supply chain for a small fashion start-up that is wholesaling its product twice a year to boutiques, independent retailers, and department stores.

The process starts with defining your business strategy—what it is you aim to do. This will be your fashion label's raison d'être, and every other activity you undertake should always be carried out with this in mind. From here you will research your market, including customers and product, to help develop your collections. Only when you have done the research should you move on to the design development stage, when the aesthetics of your range will start to become apparent. For many labels the sampling stage, when two-dimensional

4.SAMPLING

designs are turned into three-dimensional prototypes, runs alongside the design development stage. Once samples have been developed, the wholesale selling season can begin. Orders will be taken and your collection will need to go into production ready for delivery to the stores. While your production is underway, your PR and marketing for the season's collection should begin in earnest to ensure you are achieving the press you need to entice customers. Once the product lands in-store the retail sales period starts, giving the consumer access to your product and, you hope, leading to high sales and profits for the retailers. Good sales of your product will lead to reorders for next season.

As you move through the chapters of this book, each stage of the supply chain should become more apparent and the key elements for each stage will be explained in greater depth.

5.WHOLESALE SEASON SELLING

6.PRODUCTION

8.PR & MARKETING

7.DISTRIBUTION

The supply chain will play a massive part in your fashion business and your management of it will go a long way towards determining the success of your label

9.RETAIL SELLING SEASON

Case Study: Noir

Peter Ingwersen set up Noir Illuminati II in February 2005 at the age of 41. Having studied design in his native Denmark, Peter did a stint as Brand Manager for Levi's before becoming Managing Director at renowned Danish brand Day Birger et Mikkelsen. He left the relative safety of developing others' brands to follow his dream of launching "a sophisticated, edgy, and ethical luxury brand for women aged 30-plus and at a luxury entry price, targeting international leading department stores and boutiques." Within his first season Noir would be represented in Harvey Nichols (London), Lane Crawford (Hong Kong), Podium (Moscow), and 30 other prestigious retailers around the world. After three years, the number of stores stocking Noir has almost doubled and Peter is discussing proposals for his first retail outlet.

Peter's vision for his label stems from his desire "to show the world that ethics and style can go hand in hand" and "to be the first brand to turn corporate social responsibility sexy." He recognized that there was beginning to be a change in consumers' behavior, resulting in a demand for more meaningful fashion, "where the rules of the fashion industry were obeyed but with a social responsibility across the full supply chain." He set out to create what he felt the fashion industry was missing, a collection that bridged the gap between "style and ethics," and the result was a merger of two concepts: Noir, Peter's vision for a luxury brand, and Illuminati II, his luxurious fabric brand that supplies the highest quality cotton fabrics to Noir and other luxury brands under the umbrella of the United Nations' Global Compact principles (*www.unglobalcompact.org*) and the International Labor Organization (*www.ilo.org*). "Illuminati II's vision is to deliver organic and fair trade cotton fabrics while ensuring sustainability of the Humane Business Model from the heart of Africa."

Peter manufactures the Illuminati II cotton fabric in Europe, using raw cotton sourced from Uganda. Peter pays above industry prices for the raw cotton in an attempt to revive the industry and to create sustainable economic growth in the region. He has established the Noir Foundation, which uses a percentage of earnings to fund essential medicine and micro loans. As a result, "Noir is able to offer collections for both consumer fashion and social conscience by creating meaningfulness in the luxury segment." He is adamant that "it's not more expensive to create beautiful, ethically correct clothing; it's just a lot more hassle, and if you take an ethical approach you need a different supply chain. But, fundamentally, you can't persuade people to join in the ethical challenge unless you give them really sexy, stylish clothes."

The first Noir collection had a total of 60 pieces and was funded out of Peter's own pocket. Having targeted the luxury end of the market, key price points included trouser suits at €1,150, cotton shirts at €230, silk blouses at €390 and dresses at €850. After the success of the first season, Peter was able to attract investment into the business to help it grow and says it has taken three years to break even. Peter says that "investment is a must if you want to match your ambitions with your growth." He believes that a certain amount of novelty and hype helped to achieve Noir's initial success, but also says the people he works with and his motivation to make a difference have played an enormous part. He sees the ability to be strategic and position your brand, together with financial acumen and networking skills, as essential to running a successful fashion label.

"Noir is sophisticated, edgy, sexy, luxurious, and stands for corporate social responsibility, and these key messages need to be transmitted to the end consumer via the media." In order to achieve this, the Noir collection, high-quality Noir images, a press show, and the Noir story are carefully crafted to allow for media awareness, which can ultimately be translated into business opportunities. Peter explains: "Noir secured a four-page article in US *Harper's Bazaar* before even hitting the stores. This strong support gave immediate credibility to the brand and enabled Noir to attract retailers."

Noir offers high-end luxurious designs that are style-driven but underpinned with a socially responsible message

*W*hat is it that makes being your own boss so attractive and how can you make sure that you are in the best position, before you start spending money, to overcome any obstacles that will be thrown your way? This chapter examines some of the main benefits of setting up on your own as well as looking at the first steps you should consider taking. It also looks at the benefits of setting objectives to help you achieve your ultimate goal of running your own fashion label.

Going Solo

Why is it that so many people have the same dream of packing in their nine-to-five job to set up their own business?

1 *Freedom:* You're the boss. That means you set the rules. No more asking permission for time off and, more importantly, you gain the freedom to set your own goals.

2 *Creativity/vision:* The opportunity to develop something from scratch exactly as you envisage it, and the possibility of creating a lasting legacy.

3 *Control:* The final word is yours and the success of the venture lies in your hands.

4 *Choice:* Mac or PC, nine-to-five or ten-to-six, orange or white walls: your own taste and style can dictate those of the company.

5 *Ambition:* Your company can be as big as you are able to make it; however, if you want to stay small, you can.

6 *Financial reward:* There is no ceiling on your potential earnings.

7 *Working from home:* Many new small fashion labels are set up from home. That means no more wasted time commuting.

8 *Choice of personnel:* You can hire the people you want to work with.

9 *Long holidays:* You can take as much time off as you want, whenever you want.

10 *Flexibility:* Your great ideas can be implemented whenever you think they're ready.

Although these are common reasons for setting up your own business, for every positive there is a negative, and you need to think about these just as carefully. They include:

1   **Lack of support:** Often you have no one to turn to when questions arise that are beyond your experience. Lack of support can be a real issue, especially in the early days, when finances may not permit full- or even part-time employees.

2   **The buck stops with you:** You're the boss and the company's success will initially be down to the decisions you make and the work you put in. Your company is therefore only as strong as the skills you bring to the table.

3   **Financial insecurity:** When suppliers are demanding payment and there is only a limited amount in the bank you will be the last to get paid. If the venture fails, any financial investment you have put in will be lost.

4   **Working 24/7:** Your business becomes a full-time venture even when you're not at the studio. Switching off can be very difficult when there is so much to do.

5   **Stress:** Running your own business, especially one as demanding as a fashion label, can be extremely stressful.

6   **Loneliness:** Setting up your own business, particularly if you are working alone from home, can be isolating. If you are used to working in a business environment, being on your own can be a shock to the system.

7   **Lack of motivation:** The only boss checking over your shoulder to make sure you are meeting your targets will be you. If you are not a self-starter, deadlines can quickly slip and problems with your business will arise.

8   **Swapping one boss for many:** Although you may technically be the boss of the company you are still answerable to your customer base. In effect, you may be swapping one boss for many!

==

QUICK TASK   Take 5 minutes

Make a list of all the positives you can think of for setting up your own fashion label and then a list of all the negatives. Do the positives outweigh the negatives?

==

Before Setting up in Business

Once you have decided that being your own boss is definitely what you want to do, you need to start focusing your ideas. Here are ten things to think about right from the start. You should give careful consideration to each. They will also be discussed in more detail on the following pages.

1 **Assess yourself:** You are the key to the success of the business. What are your strengths and what areas do you need to develop? Ask others what they think your strengths are.

QUICK TASK Take 5 minutes

Make a list of all the key attributes/personality traits you think are needed to be a successful entrepreneur. Assess yourself against this list. How many attributes do you think you possess? Now give the list to a friend or family member and see how they assess you against it.

---

2 **Have a word:** Talk to as many people as you can to get advice. Speak with other business owners and find out what their experiences have been. The more aware you are of the challenges ahead, the better you can prepare.

3 **Make sure there is a business opportunity:** The quickest way to fail is to have a product or service that nobody wants!

QUICK TASK Take 10 minutes

Do a SWOT analysis (see page 108)—take your business idea and make a list of all the strengths, weaknesses, opportunities, and threats surrounding it. Weigh up the positives against the negatives to establish if it's really as good an idea as you first thought.

---

4 **Research the market:** Just because you think your idea is great doesn't mean others will. You need to research your potential customers' needs and wants as well as their spending habits.

5 **Get relevant experience:** If you want to open a retail store, then work for one first. How will you know what the demands of the fashion and lifestyle sector will be if you've never worked in that arena? It can also give you an understanding of how store buyers plan their seasonal spending budgets and source new labels.

6 **Put it down in a plan:** Keep a notepad with you at all times. Write down any great ideas or potential obstacles. You can start to formulate your ideas and bring to life what's in your head. Eventually this can be developed into a more structured business plan.

7 **Build relationships:** Building strong and lasting relationships is essential for any business. Start early, especially with your bank. Get them on your side. Belief in you and your idea now will help when cash flow gets tight later. You will also need to start thinking about how you can start to build a relationship with your customer base.

8 **Get support:** It is imperative to get the support of friends and family around you. They need to understand the demands placed on your time. Their

support will be crucial, especially when the going gets tough. You will also need specialized support for your fashion business, ranging from pattern cutters to printers, and from stylists to photographers. Start developing this base early so that when the need arises you don't waste precious time searching for the right person.

9 **Seek professional advice:** You will need a good attorney and accountant. Take time to find them and make sure they are small business specialists. Their professional advice can be the difference between success and failure.

10 **Remember—money in, usually less; money out, always more:** It is quite common for new business owners to overestimate their projected income and underestimate costs. While being optimistic is part and parcel of being an entrepreneur, being prudent when making your initial forecast may save your blushes later.

Setting Objectives

Setting specific objectives will help focus your business idea and allow you to plan your activities. When drawing up your list—or even when thinking about going solo—some of your objectives will be personal (wanting a better standard of living, freedom of expression, or more money), while others will be business-oriented (getting your product in the pages of a leading magazine, stocking in five major stores during your first season, or turning over a set figure in the first year). It is important to distinguish between the two when assessing your priorities for the business, as your objectives may sometimes be in conflict with each other. A personal objective of wanting to spend more time with your family may be in direct conflict with a business objective of looking for the company to break even within the first 18 months, since it is very likely that this will necessitate working extremely long hours. Be aware at the beginning of exactly what you want to achieve.

Before you start setting out your objectives you need to understand the difference between an objective and a goal. Goals are somewhat vague general aspirations that are not specific enough to be measured, such as "I want to be the best fashion designer in the world." Try to avoid setting goals.

Objectives, on the other hand, are specific. They can be output objectives, or they can be attitudinal or behavioral. But, most of all, they are measurable and concise. You can touch an object; it's there, it's actual and it's finite. "I want to be selected designer of the year by *Vogue* magazine." Try to set objectives and write them down. The act of writing them down puts in place the plan for their achievement.

Being your own boss is not for everyone and there are many factors to consider before taking the plunge. However, for the many who take this path the positives usually outweigh the negatives and it's a choice they wished they had made sooner. The case studies throughout the book show that for most people, setting up their own label was something they knew they just had to do.

===

TASK Give yourself 30 to 40 minutes to complete steps 1 to 6

STEP 1: Take an A4 sheet of paper and draw a vertical line down the center. On the left side write the heading **Personal Objectives**, and on the right side the heading **Business Objectives**. At the very top, in the center, write the heading **Immediate Objectives**.

STEP 2: Take ten minutes to list as many personal objectives as you can think of and write them in the left-hand column. Remember, personal objectives are to do with achieving the lifestyle you want.

STEP 3: Take another ten minutes to do the same for your business objectives and write these down in the right-hand column. Remember that these objectives are directed at the way you want the business to develop, for example to pick up five key stockists in your first season, or to employ a design assistant to free up your time for other areas of the business.

STEP 4: See if there are any conflicts between your personal and business objectives, or even between objectives in the same column. Ideally, your business objectives should support your personal ones.

STEP 5: Choose three personal objectives and two business ones, and try to develop them in more detail. Write them down in the first person future tense—"I will achieve… ." Make sure you include a date by which each objective will be achieved.

STEP 6: Take a separate piece of paper and print each statement of intent in order of priority.

STEP 7: When you wake up in the morning read your list aloud, then close your eyes and picture the achievement of each objective. Imagine the feeling of seeing your collection hanging on the rails of your first stockist, taking a bow at the end of your first catwalk show, or relaxing on a Caribbean island. Then put the list away and go about your daily business with confidence.

STEP 8: Every time you achieve an objective, tick it off your list and take some time to acknowledge your achievement. Replace the objective achieved with a new one and write out a fresh list. Continue the process.

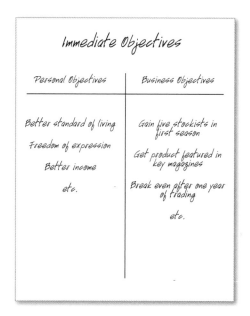

It is important that the list should not be shown to anyone unless they are working with you directly to help you meet your objectives. Achieving your objectives will mean focus and hard work and you can do without the pressure of having others assessing you on what you have and have not achieved to date. By writing down your objectives and visualizing them being achieved, you will begin to find that ideas for fulfilling them will simply come to you. When they do, act on them at once. You will find yourself moving towards running the type of fashion business you imagined.

===

Interview with Ravi Mattu, Editor of the "Business Life"
section of the Financial Times

What makes a good leader in business?

There is no fixed answer for this but a few key qualities stand out. For someone starting a business I would divide it into two key skill-sets: the ability to engage and the ability to empower.

First and foremost, you need to be a champion who can woo anyone you meet and convince them of your vision. Whether you are talking to potential funders or potential star recruits, you have to be able to inspire. This means you need to have a strong short- and long-term vision for the business you are heading. What are you trying to achieve and where do you want to be in five years?

Second, you need to be able to articulate and communicate that across your organization, from the people you manage directly to the sales rep trying to convince stores to buy your clothes to the assistant selling your dress to a consumer. This in turn will empower them to make smart decisions that will be good for the business.

For a good example of how to do this well, think of Apple. Steve Jobs was always very clear on what the company should be: a manufacturer of products that are desirable and also make your life easy. From the way its products are designed to the high level of customer service you get at an Apple Store, this key premise resonates across the brand right from the top to the bottom of the purchasing chain.

Third, and most important, you need to carry your people with you. It is a cliché but a leader should be working to create a culture that doesn't merely rely on him or her to survive. This means talking to people throughout the business and listening to what they have to say. You need to take soundings from the ground up to really understand what is happening in any organization you lead. It is also a great way of identifying the key people within your organization.

This means never forgetting to keep it human. Always remember that whatever technology, hierarchy, and management systems you might use, leadership is about managing and dealing with people. Unless you communicate with them directly, you will never be a good leader.

In your experience, what makes a successful business partnership within the creative industries? What should a start-up be looking for in their fellow business partners?

Many people start businesses with a partner partly because of the confidence effect: it is easier to be bold and ambitious if someone is on the journey with you than if you are on your own. In creative industries, the most successful partnerships have often been between quite different personalities. Think of Yves St-Laurent and Pierre Bergé, Valentino Garvani and Giancarlo Giametti, or even Paul McCartney and John Lennon. In each case, the partners had a counterbalancing effect on the other with the result that the work they produced as a team was better than what they might have been able to achieve alone.

In creative industries, this can be crucial in ensuring that the work of an artistic genius is commercially viable, too. One partner concentrates on the aesthetic, the other on making money from it. So, in an ideal world you would be looking for someone whose skills do not simply mirror your own but complement them. However, you should have a similar perspective on what makes a business work both in the big picture sense (you have a shared vision of what you want the business to be and ultimately achieve) and also on the more mundane aspects of business life (a similar work ethic, for example, so that neither person feels he/she is carrying more of the load than the other, which is certain to create resentment).

What works depends invariably on which stage you are at in your business. So, the person you start out with might be the right one to get things off the ground but as you get bigger or find yourself in challenging conditions you may discover that you are jarring more than jiving. Just like a marriage, you have to work at any partnership; you may need occasionally to get some outside guidance to make sure it's the right relationship for your business and, if necessary, be able to live through a divorce if the sustainability of the business demands it.

In a nutshell: don't look for a mirror image of yourself; be flexible; and analyze constantly.

How important is it for a business to adapt continually?

Anyone setting out to create a business ought to bear in mind the famous words of economist JM Keynes: "When the facts change, I change my mind." You may start out with a very fixed idea of what you want your business to be and convince yourself that once you have overcome a set of challenges, you will find yourself in the promised land of commercial success. The reality, however, is that building a business is a bit like standing on quicksand—the ground beneath you is constantly shifting and you need to be able to adjust continually to changing circumstances.

For entrepreneurs, this can be difficult. On the one hand, you need to be driven by a clear goal that you are passionate about. At the same time, along the way, you need to know when to tweak and/or veer from the vision when conditions demand it. If you are starting a business you need to be prepared to change tack as the "facts" change. Whether that means rethinking the type of business you are, changing your branding, or deciding when to expand or cut back, from time to time you need to be able to stand back and assess your business honestly and be open to change if things aren't going as planned. And remember: lots of creative people have a good idea for a business, but few have the flexibility and ability to adapt to changing conditions that enable them to build a successful enterprise.

You could say that running a business is a bit like being a surfer—you need to adjust to the wave rather than believing that standing up is an end in itself.

Case Study: Yasmin Kianfar

Yasmin Kianfar completed a BA in Fashion Design with Marketing at Central St Martins in London before setting up her eponymous label in 2010 at the age of 23. The label focuses on luxury contemporary womenswear with product retailing between $400 to $2,400. Yasmin knew she wanted to launch straight after she graduated. Her desire to use her final year to work on her own label didn't always sit well with her tutors. "I was striving to combine innovation with commerciality and they wanted to see pure innovation."

Yasmin's launch collection was spring/summer 2011. "I made the collection eveningwear as I felt there was more room for impact as an emerging designer in this area." Yasmin used neutral colors including black, white, camel, and nude, which meant the collection could suit any season. "I did this intentionally," Yasmin explains, "as I had no idea if I would be successful with buyers immediately."

Yasmin's sales strategy was "to get the attention of key industry players and buyers to secure an order." She "cold called the stores and explained I was a new designer and wanted to send the buyers my lookbook." This approach led to an order from the prestigious Browns Focus boutique. "I kept my focus incredibly narrow at first. I knew I wanted to sell at Browns from the outset and they were the first buyers I contacted." Yasmin then contacted buyers from similar stores internationally. These included Opening Ceremony, 10 Corso Como, Luisa Via Roma, and Colette. "I knew that it would be a waste of time contacting the department stores before I was more established."

Yasmin says, "I do not believe I would have had the same success if I had waited a year after graduating. There is definitely a strong desire from boutiques for something entirely new." She believes it is important to play on your newness as you only have one shot. She benefited from being so focused on her intended stockists while developing the collection, as rejection is demoralizing in the early stages of business.

For her second season Yasmin focused on retaining the stockists she had rather than looking to grow too quickly. This included visiting Opening Ceremony in New York and developing relationships with buyers rather than spending on a trade show.

Yasmin samples and manufactures her product in London "with a few different individuals who do small unit production for me." She believes this works well because she "can request any quantity and can manage it tightly. I will try wherever possible though to manufacture in the UK, for both ethical and practical reasons."

One of Yasmin's key marketing tools is her seasonal lookbook, "a necessary expense for my target customer." She believes it's important not to start showing on the catwalk unless you have the funding to continue to show from then on. "You can't start and then stop, otherwise it looks like you failed." However she does not rule out using the catwalk as business expands.

Yasmin handled the PR for her label from day one and although she now has agency representation believes it is still important for new designers to do it themselves in the first few years. "The editors and bloggers want to hear from you as the designer, initially." Yasmin also says that while PR is important, sales should be the focus in the beginning. "Sales buy you time in the business to work on your PR. It doesn't work in reverse and ultimately your time is precious when you start out—you have to prioritize."

Yasmin runs the label on her own with the help of one or two interns and admits that "working on your own is lonely and you need to manage your environment to suit you." She believes it's important for graduates to "be realistic as to whether you want to be a designer or run your own label, the vast majority of your time will not be spent designing and you need to enjoy the other aspects equally." She is incredibly self-driven and says part of her motivation for setting up was to be "completely independent. I don't believe the same opportunities are there for designers/employees working under a brand."

Yasmin Kianfar aimed to be self-employed from the start of her career

Chapter 3: Business Legal Structure

*A*ny individual or group of individuals who wish to start a business should consider the most appropriate legal structure to use. New York law recognizes four basic forms of business organization, all of which have different strengths and weaknesses: sole proprietorship, business corporations, limited liability companies, and partnerships. Adopting the appropriate structure from the outset is important and it is prudent to seek the advice of an attorney before making your choice.

Sole Proprietorship

This is the most basic business organization. A sole proprietor is someone who is engaged in business on his own account, without any form of legal entity, corporation or partnership, involved. This form of business organization does not shield the sole proprietor from business liabilities for which he shall respond personally. A sole proprietorship lasts only as long as its owner, so his death or retirement will bring the business to an end. Sole proprietorship, however, is significant from a tax perspective, as it allows income generated by, or expenses incurred in, the business activity to be treated as business, as opposed to individual, income and expenses.

How to Set Up
There are no legal formalities, except for registering it with the Internal Revenue Service (IRS), and obtaining the required Tax ID number, necessary to open bank accounts and to file tax returns. However, if the sole proprietorship intends to conduct business under an assumed name ("doing business as" [dba]), then a Certificate of Assumed Name must be filed with the County Clerk for the County where the business is located.

Liability
This business model should not be employed for anything beyond an undemanding simple business, since a sole proprietor is not protected from full personal liability.

Management and Raising Finance
As a sole proprietor you are the business, so you will make all the decisions on its day-to-day running. Sole proprietors will inject some of their own finance into the initial set-up of the business. Attracting further investment by third parties will be difficult, as a sole proprietorship is organized to accommodate only the proprietor's stake. Financing through bank loans will depend on the availability of assets guaranteeing the loan.

Conceptual shoe by Gil Carvalho

Taxation

All profits that the sole proprietorship makes are yours directly, without further corporate process or formality. Business income is reported on the owner's individual tax return, eliminating the need to file two separate returns, and so are the business expenses, reported as deductions from income.

Business Corporations

The most common type of corporation in New York is the business corporation, formed under section 402 of the Business Corporation Law (BCL). A business corporation is designated by the suffix "Inc." or "Corp."

How to Set Up

You should consult an attorney to file a Certificate of Incorporation with the Department of State in Albany and to prepare the other documents you will require—usually the Certificate of Incorporation, the issuance Shares of Corporate Stock (reflecting the value, capital contribution, and ownership, in whole or in part, of the corporation), the By-Laws (setting forth the internal rules and policies, as well as the authority and restrictions on powers of any appointed Director and Officer), a Shareholders' Agreement (if more than one shareholder), and, of course, the necessary Resolutions, expressing the deliberated will of the corporation, through its Board of Directors, to act or perform certain transactions (e.g. to issue or sell the stock, appoint Officers, ratify contracts and tax returns).

Liability

A business corporation protects the members (shareholders) from personal liability for the corporation's debts. Subject to certain exceptions (often arising from fraudulent trading or other acts done in bad faith) the law treats a corporation as a different "person" from its ownership. The business corporation itself remains liable for its debts and can be made to pay them from all or any of its assets.

Corporate Governance

Once the shareholders have acquired the shares of the corporation, they appoint the Director(s) to serve on the Board of Directors, the governing body of the entity. The Board will appoint Officers, such as President, Treasurer, and Secretary, who will execute the directives and instructions of the Board. The Officers, for all intents and purposes, run the corporation's day-to-day affairs. (It is common to alter those titles or add others, such as Chief Executive Officer, Operating Officer, or Financial Officer. This is really a cosmetic issue.)

Although the law will not fasten shareholders, directors, or officers with personal liability, care must be taken to comply with all the "corporate formalities." The corporation should employ the services of a corporate agent to remind the directors/officers when documents need to be filed, when a meeting needs to be held, if any litigation has commenced against the corporation, and so forth. If attention is not paid to the corporate formalities, this can lead to it being cancelled; an aggressive creditor could attempt to "pierce the corporate veil," by arguing that the corporation is a mere shell and that the creditor should be permitted to pursue the ownership personally for the corporation's debts. A corporation can last forever, or for any term of years set out in its Certificate of Incorporation. This means that continual vigilance over the long term is necessary to make sure formalities are respected and the business is properly run.

Raising Finance

Forming a business corporation may assist when it comes to raising capital. However, many investors, banks in particular, will often insist on a personal guarantee before loaning money to small, new corporations, as will landlords when leasing office or retail space. Be prepared in the early stages to provide guarantors for any loans made. Lenders can be given a higher degree of security by being granted preferred stock/shares or debentures as security for their loan. Such security means that in the event of insolvency, the holders of such paper are paid before unsecured creditors. However, if things have gone badly financially, this may not mean much. In a fashion company, the main assets will typically be the intellectual property (trade names and brands [trademarks], the designs), and, of course, the designer. When such assets are valued because of their performance in the marketplace, investors will be interested in financing to the extent that the intellectual property is pledged (by pledging the shares of stock) or the designer legally bound to the employment of the corporation.

Taxation

Business corporations in the United States file and pay their own federal and state taxes on income and must file taxes every year. Shareholders will be paid dividends upon the distributed profits, which must be reported as taxable income (profits) by the corporation and declared as personal income on the shareholders' own personal tax returns: taxes are paid twice on the same income. This problem may be avoided or mitigated in a number of ways (it is important that an accountant participates in the planning of the corporate formation)—payment of bonuses or salary increases will reduce or eliminate any taxable corporate profits. A business corporation may elect to be treated as a "sub-chapter S corporation," which is taxed like a partnership—see page 37—and requires certain filings with the IRS.

Limited Liability Company (LLC)

The Limited Liability Company (LLC) has characteristics that belong both to business corporations and also to partnerships. It is flexible and affords members liability protection and promotes capital accumulation by reducing the burden of taxation. An LLC is, however, quite costly to form.

How to Set Up
In New York an LLC is formed by filing Articles of Organization (signed by one or more of the organizers) with the state. There is a publication requirement, which means the organizers have to pay for six weeks of press advertisements, alerting the world to the formation of the LLC. These advertisements must appear in a newspaper designated by the County Clerk and published in the County where the LLC will have its place of business, and can be expensive.

Liability
An LLC gives its members (i.e. shareholders) the same protection as a business corporation. Accordingly, a member is personally liable only to the extent of his shares. The LLC is liable for its business debts to the full extent of its assets. Formalities must be observed and careful attention should be paid to the preparation of the Articles of Organization and the Operating Agreement, which govern what the LLC can legally do and the rights and obligations of members and managers. Such documents have to be crafted to the particular needs of the business.

Management and Raising Finance
The governance and maintenance of the LLC is less demanding than that of the business corporation, with nearly no record-keeping requirements. The owners are defined as Members, the executives as Managers. There is no Board of Directors.

Taxation
An LLC consisting of two or more members can opt to be taxed on the same basis as a partnership. This means the LLC pays no taxes on its own income and taxes are paid only by those individuals who receive dividends or salaries. Alternatively, any LLC can ask to be taxed like a corporation. A one-member LLC can also be taxed as a sole proprietorship, in effect ignored for tax purposes, with its single member recording the LLC's income as his own on his personal tax return. The taxation basis for LLCs allows them to accumulate capital free of tax (i.e. on money not distributed).

You could establish your business as a Limited Liability Company like Knomo, which is costly to form but very flexible

Partnerships

There are two principal types of partnership—the "general partnership" and the "limited partnership (LP)." The partnership is a legal entity, which can sue or be sued in its own name. If it is to trade under a business name, it must file a Certificate of Assumed Name with the relevant County Clerk.

How to Set Up
A partnership is founded on a contractual arrangement between two or more partners, and recognized by the IRS for tax purposes. The first stage is to draft a Partnership Agreement, in consultation with a lawyer. Without a written agreement, or with an agreement that lacks terms or clarity, the New York statute will provide the necessary terms by default, and the partners may not like what the law imposes upon them.

Liability
In a general partnership, all the partners are in it together. If the business fails and has debts, and there are three partners, two of whom have nothing and the third of whom is rich, the rich one will be liable to pay the entire amount.

Every limited partnership, on the other hand, has one general partner, who remains fully personally liable for all partnership debts. The limited partner's liability is limited to the extent of his capital contributions to the limited partnership. Often, a limited partnership will use and appoint a business corporation, of nominal value, as its general partner. Creditors can pursue the general partner for all its wealth, but if it is a ten-dollar corporation that will not get them far.

All partners owe one another "fiduciary duties"—they must not steal from one another, deny each other the proper rewards for efforts made, or "divert partnership opportunities." So, if partners A and B discover that partner C has been diverting partnership business away from the partnership for C's benefit, A and B can sue C for breach of his fiduciary duty. Partnerships last for as long as the partners wish—or until a "dissolution event," usually spelled out in the Partnership Agreement, occurs.

Taxation
Both types of partnership are totally disregarded for taxation purposes and pay no taxes on their own income. The members, however, must account for and pay taxes on the money distributed to them.

Other Ways of Starting a Fashion Business

License to retail

If you are looking to buy into the success of an already established business, then a license to retail might well be for you. Unlike a traditional license (to design, manufacture, and distribute products, see Chapter 11, page 139), under a license to retail an established fashion business grants you the right to operate a retail store under its brand name and trademark, using its established architecture and interior design, and selling solely products under that trademark. The consumer entering such a licensed store will perceive it as an integral part of the fashion business's operation.

The license to retail is a different type of operation from a franchise, a form of agreement that may be counterproductive to a fashion house's plans. A franchise is governed by a separate and complex body of specific laws and is an arrangement that is usually peculiar to the service and restaurant industry. The franchise arrangement provides three elements: the use of a trademark; the payment of a fee (a royalty); and the exercise of control by the franchisor over the retailer. Fundamentally, in a franchise the retailer is simply an investor who has no right to exercise any "business judgment" as all details of the franchised retail operation will be controlled and provided by the franchisor/licensor to assure absolute uniformity among all units in the retail network.

Remember:

Although what is written here has New York in mind, the rules and principles are generally applicable throughout the United States. However, never take any step without legal advice. When going into business in fashion, starting a new label and taking huge risks, it would be best to minimize the personal financial dangers. The safest entities through which to trade are probably the LLC, the business corporation, or the limited partnership. The sole proprietorship or general partnership should be avoided.

In contrast to the franchise arrangement, in the license to retail it is rare for the fashion house to request payment of an additional fee by the licensed retailer; instead it will secure a long-term commitment. To avoid triggering the franchise legislation, the licensing fashion house will disclaim the right to control the retail operation or deprive the retailer of any business judgment, allowing freedom to—for example—price the products, schedule sales and discounts, choose the hours of operation, and decide how to display the product. Without this latitude a fashion retailer's business could be significantly impaired.

James Montgomery, Esq. and Giacomo Corrado, Esq.
Corrado Montgomery, New York

Case Study: Knomo

Howard Harrison (former lawyer and investment banker), Benoit Rescue (former creative director in advertising), and Alastair Hops (former retail banker) set up Knomo in October 2004, specializing in luxurious and stylish workbags and accessories for urban professionals. Howard explains: "The idea for the brand came about after traveling with the standard, ugly black laptop bags and having my bag mistaken for someone else's at Heathrow Airport. I realized there was a gap in the market for a stylish, fashion-led laptop bag and so Knomo was born."

Knomo launched with six initial styles and a total range of 18 pieces, focusing on leather laptop bags that offered functionality while not sacrificing style. Since then the company has grown rapidly and the product range has expanded to offer a wide range of men's and women's bags and laptop cases as well as small accessories, including iPod covers. Retail price points range from £26 to £250.

The business was self-financed for the first three years with the directors each making an initial investment to get the business off the ground and deciding not to take anything out of the company for the first two years of operation. They were able to further finance the company by securing an overdraft from their bank, as well as a loan through the government-backed Small Business Loan Scheme. Cash flow was further eased by applying for debt funding in the form of trade (import) and invoice finance. Alastair warns, "Manage your cash flow carefully as cash is king, and make sure you have a friendly and understanding banker."

It took Knomo 15 months of trading to break even, and they believe their website (*www.knomo.com*) has been an important contributor to the total revenues of the business. The decision to reinvest all funds back into the business in order to grow it internationally means they do not expect any profits in the next two to three years.

They had a very focused sales strategy for the domestic UK market and for introducing the brand globally. "In the UK we have followed a wholesale model and were very targeted with the retailers that we wanted to stock Knomo and approached retailers directly (not through a trade show). In the first 12 months we listed Knomo at all premium department stores in the UK except for Harrods, which was added in 2006. We have not to date marketed ourselves aggressively to independent retailers and boutiques."

Within the first 18 months they took the product to trade shows in France and Germany but say that this proved to be too early for the brand. In their second year they started to work with distributors in key overseas markets and believe they have had about a 50 percent success rate with their distribution partners. They also recognized that the US represented the largest market for their type of product and spent 12 months researching how they could enter it successfully. Having met a number of potential distribution partners and considered launching in the US on their own, they decided the best option would be to form a joint venture with an experienced US partner. Howard says, "We have recently established a joint venture in the United States and have taken some investors on board to fund this business. We license the product to this joint venture and have a 50 percent share in the business."

Knowing when to work with and listen to others, and an ability to network have been of vital importance to Knomo. "With no experience in the sector, we have learnt a great deal from listening to experts in the industry, retailers, and consumers." Their tip for successful networking is "always make an effort to speak to as many people as possible, ask lots of questions and have fun!"

This ability to network has been combined with a truly innovative product, and Knomo consider that these are the two main reasons for their brand's success so far. They believe it is essential to make sure you have a USP (unique selling point): "If you don't stand out you will never get noticed. We have managed to combine clever design with innovative functionality. Without great product, there is no business." Ultimately they are looking to "create a global brand that is fun, distinctive, and synonymous with cool workbags", and are driven by a "passion for creating great products and the challenge of reinventing a sector that is traditionally staid and boring."

Starting with designer laptop cases, Knomo have gradually increased their product range as the business has expanded

JIMMY CHOO
LONDON

Chapter 4: What's in a Name?

A great name is the beginning of a great brand. The best name for your brand is one that customers can easily remember and associate with you. Your brand name can also be protected as a trademark. In the fashion industry it is particularly important to get your name and logo right, as they are such an integral part of creating your overall brand image. This chapter will take you through the process of choosing a name and designing your logo. Before you begin, however, it is important to understand that you need to consider at least two, and possibly three, names for your company. The first is the brand name, also known as the "mark," "label," or source "identifier." The second is the trade name, the name under which the business is conducted and is applicable if the business is incorporated in some way (see Chapter 3). Finally, the third is the domain name, which is used for your website.

Brand Name

The brand name is an identifier for your product and is by far the most important of the three names. It is the "mark" used to distinguish your product from those of another business so that consumers are not confused. Your choice of name is important for many reasons:

✖ Quite often it is the first thing your customers come in contact with

✖ Your name is your most visible attribute

✖ It will be the cornerstone of all your marketing materials, from the storefront, to carrier bags, swing tickets, and lookbooks

✖ Your name portrays your label's personality, so you want it to stand out and be easily recalled.

The first step is to look at the competition and see if there are any trends that you should be taking into consideration. It is very common for high-end luxury designers to use their own names, as they are the main focus behind the label. Think Marc Jacobs, John Galliano, Alexander McQueen. Each time you buy a piece from these collections you buy a piece of the designer's creativity and the name reflects this added value. By way of contrast, at the chain retail end of the market we have Gap, French Connection, Diesel, Miss Sixty. They tell us little about the designers behind the brand, but with effective

A signature brand: Jimmy Choo

marketing and advertising campaigns they have become easily remembered and reflect the type of product and the brand's personality.

The most effective names are often those that reflect the personalities of the business and its people—even if they don't describe exactly what the brand stands for. You therefore need to identify what type of image you want your brand or product to project—for example exclusive, accessible, feminine, masculine, sporty, edgy.

✖ Do you want the name to reflect your product—clothing, accessories, jewelry, etc.? Or would something more abstract be suitable?

✖ Do you want to use your own name, linking your own personality and image intrinsically with that of your label? It's worth considering here that if there is potential for investors to buy out your company, and with it your brand name, it will leave you without control of your own name in the marketplace (examples include Roland Mouret, Jimmy Choo, and Jil Sander) (see Trade Name, page 46). Also, to avoid an expensive legal fight, check that you do not have a namesake in the industry who has already established an eponymous brand.

✖ Do you want a traditional-sounding name, conveying durability and old-fashioned values, or a modern one, suggesting a fresh, innovative approach?

✖ Try to make the name instantly engaging, easy to remember, and relevant to your product.

Marks have been classified by the courts into a hierarchy of four categories: generic, descriptive, suggestive, and arbitrary or fanciful. Generic terms and/or generic uses, for example "jeans" as a mark for jeans, should be avoided as they are not distinctive and are either needed for use by others in the trade or widely used by them. Descriptive terms may, by use and advertising over time, become distinctive but this may never overcome the right of third parties to make fair, descriptive use of the word or words in question—even in a globalized market you will find markedly different treatment at the hands of trademark examiners in different countries as to what is generic or merely descriptive, the United States being quite strict. Suggestive marks are distinctive if they only "suggest" rather than describe a characteristic of your product. Fanciful and arbitrary marks are often the strongest.

Some important don'ts are:

✖ Don't make a brand name or identifier generic: for example, don't say "care for your guccis" when you mean a pair of Gucci shoes. There are plenty of others who will make use of brand names for various purposes, good or bad, so the brand owner, if no one else, should insist on good brand usage wherever he or she can. If you don't have a generic name for a branded product, invent one—VELCRO is for "hook and loop fasteners" (a reference to the two woven tapes, one with looped pile and one with hooks which are cut so that they stick to the pile).

✖ Don't adopt as a brand name anything which is arguably immoral or scandalous, deceptive, or deceptively misdescriptive, or which disparages, falsely suggests a connection with or sponsorship by another person, or

The name you choose for your fashion label will be extremely important and will be used across a number of different mediums, including bags. Take the time to get the right name for your business

brings a person or institution or religious belief or national insignia into contempt or disrepute.

✖ Don't omit to get written permission to use the name of a living person.

✖ Think about the future and don't use words or phrases that are likely to date quickly.

✖ If you're likely to be trading overseas, check that the name doesn't mean anything inappropriate in the languages of your target audience.

✖ Think about callers and customers and don't use very long names, strange wordings and unusual spellings, or names that are hard to pronounce.

✖ Don't confuse a brand name with a trade name or domain name (see below).

Protecting Your Brand Name

Once you have chosen your name, you need to register it as a trademark to prevent others using the name, for example to name a new product or service. First check that it isn't too similar to one that someone is using as a trademark. Even if you don't choose to register it as a trademark now, it may save you a lot of time and hassle in the future. Find out whether someone has already registered it by visiting the United States Patent and Trademark Office website. Go to *www.uspto.gov* and follow the link to "Trademarks" then Trademark Electronic Search System (TESS).

Registering your brand name can also be undertaken on the website. Go to *www.uspto.gov* and follow the link to "Trademarks" to find the online filing forms (TEAS) and information on fees; current processing time is about six months from the filing date of an application for a first indication of acceptance or not by an official action letter, and registration takes at least one year from filing for uncomplicated cases.

You then need to use your brand name to complete registration. Ceasing use can eventually lead to loss of rights to that name. If you are a foreign national and have a brand name registered outside the US, however, you need only file the brand name in the US (based on your home registration) and do not need to actually use it to complete registration.

For Knomo, choosing a name was not an easy task. Benoit Rescue explains, "We tried to think about what the brand would represent, while also thinking of something original for a technology-related accessories brand. 'Knomo,' a combination of 'knowledge' and 'mobility,' seemed to fit the bill as, despite being a little unusual, it seemed people remembered us all the more!"

Trade Name

As we have seen, this is the name under which your business is run. In the most elementary form of business organization, the sole proprietorship (see Chapter 3), a brand name and the name of the business or trade name might easily be the same. It is advisable, however, to adopt a form of business which offers some protection from unlimited liability. In this case the brand name and the trade name will be legally separate things even though it is usually the case that the business entity will own the brand name as part of its assets.

You may easily incorporate your business in some manner and thus adding Inc., or LLC after the name—or even operate under a partnership name—with the result that the name of the business can be presented separately (for example Gucci America, Inc. is the trade name and Gucci is the brand name). Avoid "clutter" or confusion between brand name and trade name in advertising and promotion by presenting the brand name in a distinctive manner as a mark and avoid including the trade name. If you have to include the trade name, include it in an entirely separate space on the advert.

Registering Your Trade Name

If you incorporate your business as a business corporation you will register your trade name when you file the Certificate of Incorporation with the Department of State in Albany (see Chapter 3). Likewise, if you form an LLC you will register your name when you file the Articles of Organization. The name must be distinguishable from the name of any other business corporation or LLC on file with the Department of State. For a fee of $5 you may pre-clear the name with the Department of State Division of Corporations and for a fee of $20 you may make an application for the reservation of a name prior to filing the certificate of incorporation or articles of organization. As we have seen in Chapter 3, if you wish to trade as a sole proprietor under an assumed name you must file a Certificate of Assumed Name with the County Clerk for the County where the business is located. This will prevent a company using a similar name to yours, but will not protect your brand name. A properly used brand name which is registered as a mark could be infringed by a similar trade name used by a third party, because when consumers might be confused, trademarks can trump trade names, so it is worth registering your brand name as a trademark.

Domain Name

An internet address, or uniform resource locator (URL) may be highly desirable for promotion via the internet. You will almost certainly need to create a website and email address with your company name in it, so check whether the domain name you want to use is available. The best way to protect the domain name from unfair competition from third parties is to make sure that the operative part of the address, the second level domain name between the prefix "http://www." and the ending top level domain (TLD) "com", is identical to a registered mark for the brand name, so that it might be infringement of the mark for a third party to "knock off" the second level domain name. If your name is taken don't give up—perhaps there is a variation you could use? It is quite common for people to register names in the hope of selling them later for a profit, so you may still be able to buy your chosen name. When registering your domain it is a good idea to buy a number of endings, for example .com, .net, .edu, .biz. There are two reasons for this. First, when people try to find your website they might key in any number of variations. This means that you can redirect all the other endings to your site. Second, it prevents other people registering a similar web address.

Remember, your domain name, accessible on the internet, is not the same thing as your brand name or your trade name. It is your brand name that must be registered as your trademark, your trade name which defines the legal entity that is your business, and your domain name which is your electronic address on the internet for information (passive) or for sales (active).

Overleaf
Logos play a massive part in developing the aesthetic of a brand and sustaining its image

Simplicity when developing logos is often the key for designers delivering product at the high end of the market

The End Result

You know you have come up with a successful name when a customer looks at your product, hears the name, and says "I get it." You need your customers to connect with your brand image as quickly as possible. If, from the moment they see your product, name, and logo, they understand the story behind the brand and the lifestyle it is projecting, then you have made a huge step forward in the success of your business.

Names that are distinctive, memorable, and positive will go a long way toward promoting your company or product, so put in the time and effort to find a great one. After all, it is much the same as naming your children. It's something that will be with you for ever.

Fashion Logos

Although it can be difficult to measure the impact of a logo on the overall success of a fashion business, the right logo is crucial to creating and sustaining a brand image, which is a major contributing factor to the success and profitability of a brand. A good logo should give the potential customer a general perception of the brand's products and services, and add a degree of sophistication, reliability, and authenticity.

As a new fashion label you will be fighting to get noticed, so you need to find a balance between capturing your prospective customer's attention and looking like you're trying too hard—or, worse, not trying at all. It is essential to remember your audience, plan for the future, and keep it simple. The secret to an inexpensive but effective logo is simplicity. Your logo is part of your marketing strategy; it is about communication, not just art.

Remember: your image is how people perceive your product and brand, and not just how you want it to be perceived.

Motifs
Motifs are an important element of fashion logos. The motif used should clearly communicate the style of the brand. That's why many fashion labels will just use the company's emblem or initials as motifs on their fashion logos. Examples of such logos include Ralph Lauren, Louis Vuitton, Fred Perry, and Adidas.

Fonts
Choosing the right font is critical. A lot of labels choose not to have any branding other than their name. It is the font that creates the design twist and provides distinctiveness, making your logo unique. Just as you did when choosing your company name, decide on the perception you want the customer to have of your brand.

Color
Fashion logos tend to use high-impact colors like red, black, white, or gold. Although you can use any color, it is important to consider the color of the background on which the logo will be placed. High-impact colors tend to give a positive look and feel.

Trying to develop your image is a subjective process. It may not be until the business cards are printed, the back labels are stitched in, and the swing tickets attached, that you discover that some people love it and others loathe it. That's when you'll know whether it works—or not.

Remember:

Your logo is the creative expression of your brand's identity and one of the strongest marketing tools for communicating your brand ethos to the customer.

Developing Logos

==

Malcolm Crews—*Graphic Designer/Artistic Director, NY*

Before developing your logo you first need to determine:

1 *What your product is. Casual, dress, sportswear, accessories? Female, male, male and female, kids?*
2 *Who your customer is. Build a visual of your ideal customer; a symbol of "who" the brand is.*
3 *What your price point will be. High end? Moderate? Mass market?*
4 *A point of view (POV). Have a POV for your label and stick to it.*
5 *A brand name that best tells your story. (A designer's name is not always the best option for a brand name.)*

Once you have determined these points you can start to develop. Logo design helps guide prospective customers, who may not initially see the product. Font, color, and motif can all tell a story.

Aspects to consider when developing a logo:

✖ *Do I want a logo-mark combined with a font treatment? Hire a good graphic designer or art director to help you to develop your logo. Give as much information and direction as possible. It really can help to get an outsider's take on your vision. It's easy to be "too close."*
✖ *Do I want a logo motif that can be used separately from the font treatment?*
✖ *Do I want a font treatment only?*

Readability

✖ *Ideally, your logo should be able to stand the test of time.*
✖ *Do you want a modern, retro, or classic logo?*
✖ *Serif and sans-serif fonts are an easy way to tell a brand's story and can conjure up different styles to the reader; sans-serif fonts are generally seen as "modern, clean, fast," whereas early newspapers and flyers used serif fonts.*

Font examples

Before finally deciding on a logo, check:

✖ *Does it convey the brand's image/direction?*

✖ *Is it understandable and readable?*

✖ *Is it timeless?*

✖ *Does it work for various uses: printing, embroidery, positive/negative? Is it legible at various sizes?*

Create a logo standards guide

No matter how simple or complex your logo, a standards guide is important for consistency as your brand grows and you begin to use external suppliers.

```
Logo standards example
```

✖ *Logo color will always be black or tonal.*

✖ *Size of logo, when used in signage or packaging shall never be smaller than half an inch (1.27 cm).*

✖ *When using a logo for marketing/advertising purposes, it will always appear in the bottom right-hand corner, half an inch (1.27 cm) from each edge.*

✖ *Logo should never be seen/used on the exterior of any garment, other than the swing ticket or other marketing materials.*

✖ *Type accompanying logo shall always be Helvetica bold and be no larger than half the logo size, and no smaller than one eighth of the logo size.*

font: Helvetica Inserat Roman

fig.1

Case Study: Ed Hardy

Born in Avignon in southern France, Christian Audigier was drawn to the rock-and-roll lifestyle, and looked to fashion as a means of expressing his vision to the world. He launched the Ed Hardy clothing line in 2004, a collection of vintage-inspired fashion showcasing the artwork of tattoo artist Don Ed Hardy. Don Ed Hardy is known as the godfather of tattoo, and is one of a few Westerners who studied directly under famed Japanese tattoo master Horihide.

At 19 Christian was dubbed the "King of Jeans" by *Sportswear International* magazine for his creative design work, elaborate parties, and his unprecedented denim museum in Paris, which paid homage to some of his favorite stars, including Elvis Presley and Steve McQueen. He moved to the US at a very young age, setting up his own freelance consultancy and working with Levi's, Diesel, American Eagle Outfitters, NafNaf, and Lee, among others. However it was when he joined the clothing company Von Dutch that he gained international credibility, transforming the relatively unknown brand into a global one.

After his success at Von Dutch he was looking for a new challenge. "I was looking at all these people on the street with tattoos in California, and thought, 'Why not do a T-shirt with tattoos?'" He started researching tattoo artists and Don Ed Hardy's name kept coming up. "I wasn't even sure if he was alive or not. I contacted him and he called me back and here we are today."

Christian persuaded the artist to grant him exclusive rights to the Don Ed Hardy back catalog of tattoo designs to put on clothing for worldwide distribution, using his name to promote the line. He bought all of Hardy's archives so that he could start a new phenomenon. Using the strategy that had worked so well for him at Von Dutch, Christian set about developing a global brand, including licensing deals and his own retail stores. Christian's vision is that Ed Hardy is not just a brand, but a lifestyle offering products in a broad range of categories.

Christian has always had a charismatic and colorful approach to fashion and uses an ebullient promotional strategy to good effect. While the product is always integral to the success of the brands he has developed, Christian believes that

getting celebrities to wear the clothes has boosted the brand into a household name.

An example of Christian's guerrilla marketing strategy is his wildly popular trucker hat. He started the trend by placing the caps on Britney Spears and Justin Timberlake, who at the time were constantly followed by the media and paparazzi. The trucker hat took off when photos of the celebrity couple were published.

Since then he has worked hard to develop what is believed to be one of the best little black books in the fashion industry, with a client base that includes Madonna, Kanye West, Mariah Carey, Heidi Klum, Mickey Rourke, Snoop Dogg, and Chris Brown.

Christian says, "You've got to market the product!" and getting the product seen on the right people is key. He recognizes the importance of ensuring that his designs are visible and are worn by celebrities. He understands that the paparazzi play a huge role in the promotion of his brand and that the reported bad behavior of celebrities can mirror the rock-and-roll lifestyle reflected by the Ed Hardy brand.

He also started his own brand management company, Audigier Brand Management Group. ABMG oversees several brands including Christian's own, and others including The Same Guy and Crystal Rock. His brands are sold through a network of distributors in over 40 countries, and in over 40 Ed Hardy and Christian Audigier licensed stores.

Christian Audigier bought the rights to tattoo artist Don Ed Hardy's artwork, initially putting them on to T-shirts and caps before expanding the brand across a number of different product categories

Chapter 5: Working from Home v Setting Up a Studio

*E*stablishing a good and practical working environment is essential to success. While many aspiring designers start off in their bedrooms for practical and financial reasons, there are still certain requirements for a work space. This chapter looks at the pros and cons of working at home against the cost of taking up a studio and examines how your work space may be perceived by buyers and press.

Working From Home

When starting out, keeping costs to a minimum is important to the financial stability of the business. Working from home can be a good way to save money. You will, however, need to weigh up the pros and cons to be sure that it won't actually cost your business in the long run.

Pros and Cons

==

Pros
Not having to commute; saving on rent; taking calls in your pajamas; getting up at 8:30 am and still being at work for 9:00 am.

Cons
The office can easily overflow into your living space; it can be difficult to "switch off" during evenings and weekends; there can be distractions from housemates.

==

Do You Have the Right Space?
If you have some space at home from which to work, you need to establish if it is the right space for you.

Work out how much space you will need
This will depend on the type of fashion business you are setting up. If you will be cutting your own patterns and sampling your own product you will need a lot of flat work space. If you will be selling your product directly through your website you will need to have enough storage space for your stock without infringing on the rest of the household. If you will be outsourcing everything, a desk with the bare essentials will suffice.

Allocate a dedicated work space

You should try to allocate a permanent space to your business; ideally a room rather than just a corner. A separate room will reduce the risk of distraction. You should be able to separate your work life from your personal life as much as possible and to shut the door to either as and when required.

Keep it flexible

Will your allocated space give you the flexibility you need? At times it may need to be a design studio, sales showroom, warehouse, or distribution center. The more you can move things around and make the space suit the activity, the better. When you have designated a space for your home office, take measurements so you know exactly how much space you have to play with. Sketch a layout of the room and map out where the furniture and equipment will go.

Get the lighting right

Running your own business will require high levels of energy and enthusiasm. There is nothing more likely to sap these than a badly lit work environment. Bad lighting can cause headaches, eye strain, and fatigue. Choose a space with windows that can provide some natural light—you will need good lighting to choose color palettes for your collections. Lighting the wall behind a computer monitor can reduce eye strain, while a good adjustable desk lamp can provide light in a range of different situations.

Make the right first impression

You work environment says a great deal about you and your business. Giving potential clients a tour of your entire property is not the best starting point so try to keep your office confined to an easily accessible space near the entrance. If your work environment gives the wrong impression, try meeting outside of home as much as possible, and look into hiring meeting or showroom space when needed.

Making Use of the Space

No matter how good a work space you have, you need to make the best use of it.

Be logical

Try to create a work space that will maximize your efficiency and work flow. Know where everything is and keep key functions like phones, computers, and sewing machines in your primary work space.

Be tidy

You will need to switch between job functions several times a day, so keep your work space organized. Know where everything is at all times. Labeling can help with this. At the end of each day leave the space ready for the beginning of the next.

Remember storage

Take time to think about your storage requirements. Shelves mounted on the wall provide useful storage for home office supplies and files and do not take up any floor space. You will also require drawers for trims, buttons, and fastenings, and clothes rails for your samples.

Make sure you have a designated space that will allow you to be both creative and productive. Your surroundings should inspire you

Think multi-functional

When space is an issue, buy furniture and equipment that can perform different functions. This could include an all-in-one printer, scanner, and copier, or a storage cabinet that also provides a work surface. Furniture that can be rolled out of the way is also useful.

Keep trim

Keep any unnecessary items away from your work space. This might include anything likely to distract you (such as televisions) and stop you from working efficiently. However, you will be working in a creative industry, so don't deprive yourself of things that will help to stimulate the creative juices.

The Practicalities

There are certain things to take into account in order to make the arrangement workable.

Legal and insurance

You are legally required to notify your landlord or mortgage lender that you will be working from home, as your property may now be considered semi-commercial, rendering your initial mortgage agreement invalid. There are special semi-commercial mortgages, and your lender may require you to move to one of these. Check your home insurance, as it probably doesn't cover working from home—if you expect to receive business visitors then you will probably need additional cover. Standard working from home insurance coverage can include:

✖ Business contents
✖ Employers', public, and product liability
✖ Legal expenses
✖ Business interruption protection.

Working from home optional extras can include:
- ✖ Buildings insurance—accidental damage cover for your home business area and your home
- ✖ Home contents insurance—accidental damage cover for your home contents
- ✖ Personal possessions—peace of mind if you take personal items away from home
- ✖ "All risks" on business equipment—cover for accidental loss or damage of office equipment
- ✖ Computer breakdown—covers breakdown and failure of computer equipment, or loss/damage to computer records.

Source: *www.theaa.com*

It is also worth ensuring that any particularly expensive items of equipment or product are covered. You may be able to include some or all of these in your home contents insurance. You may also want to increase your security measures if there is a great deal of expensive equipment or merchandise being stored. The more security you have, the lower your monthly premium will be.

Health and safety

You will be legally responsible for your own health and safety and that of any employees or visitors to your premises. Study the legislation. There are some simple things you can do to make your space a good one to work in. Make sure your workstation is comfortable, and that any wires or cabling are located in a safe place (to avoid tripping). Take the time to undertake a risk assessment of the premises and identify any potential hazards.

Remember:

Make sure you comply with the law regarding insurance and health and safety regulations. Keep home life and work life separate. If you are living with others, make sure they know when and where you work.

Working from a Studio/Workshop

Taking up a studio, office, or workshop space is a big step. However, at some point you will probably need to find yourself a space away from home that will allow you to conduct your business effectively.

Pros and Cons

==

Pros
A flexible work environment; separation of work and home life; a professional business address.

Cons
The cost implications of running the studio; the financial commitment of a lease.

==

Identify Your Requirements
Before you start looking for potential space, make a list of all your requirements. This streamlines the hunt for premises. The key points will be:

Function
Make a list of the key activities of your business. Your prospective space must allow all of these activities to take place. If it is a small space, does it give you the flexibility to move things around to create a different look when customers call?

Location
Think about:
✖ The length of commute from your home to the studio or to your clients or suppliers
✖ The journey your customers will have to make
✖ Transport links and access to parking.

Cost
Set a realistic budget and stick to it. It's not just the rent or mortgage you will need to think about, but also:
✖ Set-up costs for getting the space how you need it to look
✖ Additional property costs: business rates, service charges and insurance, security deposit
✖ Day-to-day running costs: gas, water, electricity, telephone, internet, and cleaning/maintenance.

Size
Keep things to a minimum. However, don't go too small, and make sure you have enough space to accommodate potential new employees or casual labor as and when required.

Services
Think about the services you will need: toilets and kitchen facilities.

Designer Karen Walker at work
in her studio

Isolation

Running your own business can be lonely, so think carefully before choosing a location that cuts you off too much from the outside world, unless that's what inspires you the most.

Security

The most affordable studios are often located in slightly less desirable areas. Think about safety and security.

Types of Space

There are many different types of work space available. Decide which one will suit you best.

Individual work spaces

Often owned by private landlords, these can range from retail premises to offices or industrial workshops. There is often room for negotiation on rent and conditions of the lease.

Professionally managed studios

The monthly fee usually includes all studio expenses from rent, business rates and services to utilities. You will usually be surrounded by creative companies—this can help with inspiration, networking, and finding potential suppliers. The security is usually good and administrative functions may be thrown in. Rent, however, tends to be a little higher and you're less likely to find a bargain.

Shared studios

If you have found a fantastic location that ticks all your boxes but is just a bit too big and expensive, you could look for similar businesses to share the space with you. This is sometimes called a "co-operative." Have an attorney draw up a contract for each tenant and draw up a set of studio rules.

Finding a Studio

There are many ways to find a studio.

- ✗ **Word of mouth:** Recommendations from friends and family or people already in the industry.
- ✗ **Business support agencies:** Enterprise agencies' listings.
- ✗ **Real estate agents:** Estate agents' commercial listings.
- ✗ **Internet:** Information from agents to business organizations and personal postings.
- ✗ **Managed studios:** Managed premises will often have a waiting list that you can put your name down on.
- ✗ **Advertising:** Ads in local stores and on e-bulletin boards for relevant fashion sites.
- ✗ **Taking a stroll:** Seeing "for rent" signs on commercial properties; talking to local business owners.

Getting the Space

Once you have found the ideal space, before you put pen to paper and sign the contract, there are some considerations.

- ✗ Negotiate with your landlord: can you get a rent reduction or arrange a rent-free period while setting up the studio?
- ✗ Check out your landlord. It's a good idea to speak to other tenants.
- ✗ Get your solicitor to check over the rental agreement. How binding is the contract and for how long are you expected to sign? Can you make it more favorable to you?
- ✗ Check whether you are responsible for service charges, power, water, and so on.

Do your homework and get an idea of the rental values of different types of property in the area.

Case Study: no added sugar

Deborah Medhurst established the childrenswear label no added sugar in 2001 after a colorful career in the London club scene running Puscha—all night club parties held in glamorous locations for London fashionistas. There were "ten years of wonderful hedonism. Then I got pregnant." Deborah set up no added sugar as she felt the childrenswear market lacked "wit, bold color, and originality. At start up I was purely looking to have some fun, keep my business-head busy, and make some pin money." Deborah initially produced 15 different slogan print T-shirt samples and drove across London showing them to her wishlist of stores. The response to the small range was overwhelming—approximately 300 pieces were ordered and Deborah's gentle pastime quickly became "an all-consuming new baby!" Within three months Deborah added a range of playsuits and a further nine months on she extended the sizing range up to five years old.

One of the key successes for no added sugar has been the readily identifiable signature and attitude that the brand exudes. "It's a saturated market. Any designer will need to have a clear identity and an understanding of their market. Product is always king; without a good product there is no business." For the first four years they mainly produced T-shirts; it wasn't until fall/winter 2007 that they launched their first seasonal line. Now no added sugar offers full collections for boys and girls from three months up to 12 years.

The first ranges were produced in England. However, within the first year as volumes increased manufacturing was moved to Portugal where 70 percent of the range is still produced today. While Deborah says "I am not a great networker and in truth probably avoid it," she does recognize that contacts have proven important in the development of the label. "One key contact was our neighbor, Philip Start of Start Boutique in London, who generously provided us with a great manufacturing contact that we still use today."

To get things moving Deborah approached a bank to borrow money, but they wouldn't give her a loan so she had to look to family members to borrow £8,000. Deborah believes it's important to "hold on to your business. We have had many opportunities to take investment over the years but held back." She does recognize that "when the time is right to

release the potential of the brand it may involve investment," but that it's important "to be clear about your goal and how you intend to get there and be totally comfortable who you partner with."

As well as wholesaling no added sugar also offered a small catalog service. Not too long after Deborah set up the online store, and without any promotion "the mail order business tripled overnight." The online shop remains a crucial part of the business today. Deborah says, "We love it still for being in touch with what the customer likes to buy (store buyers can get it wrong and tend to play safe) and obviously the margin is considerably more favorable (than wholesale) which allows us to develop our marketing campaigns." Currently no added sugar sell direct on their webshop and supply hundreds of stockists worldwide. The strategy moving forward is to open their own store, with a view to building "an even closer relationship with our customer."

Since the inception of the business they have had no real PR drive. All press they have received has been from journalists/publications approaching them directly. Deborah says "coming from a party business which is heavily about promotion we felt pretty able to handle our own marketing and I still control this today." However she felt that the online/direct business required a different skill-set and therefore they "initially employed an external marketing company to manage this but now have brought this in house."

Deborah believes that to be successful in running your own label you need to be passionate, intuitive, confident, positive, approachable, individual, cost-conscious, and work extremely hard. She believes that a lot of no added sugar's success has come from the originality and quality of the product, as well as listening to their instincts and allowing themselves to take risks where needed. Valuing the customer is also a major factor.

no added sugar is a cool, playful childrenswear line with an attitude

Chapter 6: Jack-of-All-Trades?

*B*eing your own boss within a small company means multi-tasking. In the fashion industry, in addition to all the day-to-day functions, there are some specialized roles. You need to work out how many of these you can take on and how many you will have to outsource. If you bring people in to work for you, you'll need to get up to speed on hiring and firing techniques and legislation. This chapter looks at the functions involved in the supply chain.

The Supply Chain

Taking a fashion product from initial concept to being worn by your potential customers can be complicated, and involves a variety of job functions. The overall process is known as the supply chain (see pages 18–9), and how you manage it will determine how successful your business will be. There are four main components in the supply chain: researching the market and trends; design development; production; and sales and distribution. Within each of these four areas there are several roles, and within a large organization an individual will have responsibilities that spread over a number of the aspects. The table shows the typical job functions, and where they come into play within the four stages of the supply chain.

Key Job Roles Within the Supply Chain

Step 1 Research fashion trends	Step 2 Design development	Step 3 Production	Step 4 Sales and distribution
Fashion forecaster	Designer	Production manager	Sales director
Designer	Buyer	Buyer	Merchandiser
Buyer	Merchandiser	Merchandiser	Allocator/distributor
	Pattern cutter	Designer	PR/marketing manager
	Sample machinist	Pattern cutter	Fashion photographer/stylist
	Garment/fabric technologist	Sample machinist	Fashion journalist
		Grader	Retail manager
		Garment/fabric technologist	Sales assistant
		Quality controller	

Tailor's dummies. Image by David Hardy

Each of these functions is essential to delivering the right product at the right price, time, location, and quality. You need to identify which of these roles you yourself will be able to take on board and which you may need to outsource. The earlier you can identify the areas in which you will need to bring in support to your business the earlier you can start to work out a realistic start-up figure.

Although some job functions may appear in more than one stage, for ease of reference they have been included below only where they are most involved on a day-to-day basis. For example, although sample machinists may have input at the design development stage, they are most involved in step 3 (Production) and are therefore discussed under this heading.

STEP 1: Research Fashion Trends

Fashion is all about trends. You must understand the trends that affect your target consumer, learn to identify the direction the fashion industry is moving in, and develop your product accordingly (see Chapter 8). Large fashion retailers often have a specialist fashion forecaster (such as WGSN or the Donegar Group) working with them or have access to external trend research agencies for up-to-date information.

Fashion forecaster:
- ✖ Shops the market, attends trade and fashion events, researches online trade sites
- ✖ Offers fashion designers guidance on changes in color, fabric, and shape, and analysis of social trends that will affect fashion
- ✖ Combines a knowledge of fashion design and history with consumer information.

STEP 2: Design Development

Based on your research into the market, your customers, and the trends that are being predicted you must start to develop your initial product range (see Chapter 9). Whether or not you will be the designer, you will quite often need to look at the product you are developing from a number of different viewpoints. Within a large retail company the designers will work with the buying and merchandising teams to make sure they are creating the best product for the customer. If you are taking on all of these roles yourself you must be able to develop a healthy balance between the artistic role of designer and the role of the merchandiser, who will look at the product from the point of view of the previous season's sales analysis. Avoid falling into the trap of creating a product so elaborate that it has no commercial attraction, or a product based so much on previous seasons' sales that it becomes too safe and does not offer the customer something sufficiently different.

Put yourself in the shoes of the buyers from the stores you aim to sell to and the customers who will wear your product.

Pattern cutters, sample machinists, and garment/fabric technologists are also involved at this stage to make sure design specifications can be met.

Designer:

✖ Researches trends through comparative shopping, attending fabric fairs and trade shows, as well as following media, music, and other social influences
✖ Creates storyboards and product ranges
✖ Draws up specifications for costings and sampling
✖ Sources fabric and trimmings
✖ Works with pattern cutters and sample machinists
✖ Approves samples
✖ Visits manufacturers.

Left
Fashion forecasters will research a number of places including trade shows to find current and future trends

Right
Drawing up specification sheets like those shown pinned up in the design room of the fashion brand Schumacher is a key step in the design development of fashion products

Buyer:
* Is responsible for planning the new ranges each season
* Researches trends through comparative shopping and sales analysis
* Holds regular range review meetings with senior management
* Controls the annual budget
* Sets criteria for suppliers, including price
* Ensures deadlines and delivery requirements are met
* Works out lead times to make sure the product is in store in time.

Merchandiser:
* Works alongside the buying team to forecast the next season's ranges from an analysis of the previous season's sales figures
* Helps to decide the product mix to maximize sales
* Ensures that profit margins and stock targets are met
* Is often in charge of a large budget
* Manages the supply chain, checking deliveries and monitoring relationships with suppliers
* Works closely with the distribution team to maximize in-store stock ratios.

Pattern cutter:
* Turns the designer's sketches into patterns from which samples are made—patterns will later be used for production as well
* Establishes a block (the measurements that give a collection a size structure)
* Makes an initial draft of the pattern on paper then develops a toile in fabric, making any adjustments to get the correct fit and look
* Traces the paper patterns on to hard card
* Does pattern cutting by hand or using an automated/computerized Pattern Design System (PDS).

Garment technologist:
* Makes sure that samples from manufacturers fit perfectly and that fabric is of the quality expected
* Uses technical garment-making skills to make suggestions for improvement
* Provides technical support to the buying function
* Works with suppliers to ensure production standards are maintained
* Organizes tests of materials and coordinates reports.

STEP 3: Production

Once you enter the realms of producing fashion the process becomes very technical quite quickly. If you are taking on the physical making of your product yourself you will need to have the skills to produce it to a commercial quality. If you are going to outsource your production you will be at a disadvantage when dealing with manufacturers unless you have a production manager to oversee the process.

Given the importance of quality, you cannot afford to waste time and money getting the production process wrong. Having had all the time in the world to develop your first season's samples, you will quickly find that you will be overseeing the production of one season's sales while sampling your next season's line. For this reason many small fashion labels find the production

Developing fashion products is a technical process and involves such jobs as pattern cutters (above), sample machinists (top right), and garment technologists (bottom right)

process can be the bane of their lives, so don't be surprised if you spend most of your time acting as the production manager (see Chapter 10).

Production manager:

✖ Is responsible for managing the entire sampling and production process
✖ Ensures that the product comes in on budget and is delivered on time
✖ Sources suppliers if not using in-house facilities, and negotiates prices
✖ Works with the sales team to calculate the quantities needed for production.

Fabric technologist:

✖ Develops and maintains standards for fabric in production
✖ Works with designers to ensure the fabrics meet the needs of the product in terms of quality, performance, and price.

Quality controller:

✖ Creates internal standards for product quality
✖ Oversees quality procedures
✖ May physically measure garments against specifications to make sure they are correct.

Grader:

✖ Grades patterns to develop a full size-range for each style
✖ Develops a sizing structure
✖ Works with pattern cutters and designers.

Sample machinist:

✖ Is skilled in the use of industrial sewing machines
✖ Makes up the samples from specifications and patterns
✖ Finishes off garments to a high spec.

STEP 4: Sales and Distribution

Once you have researched your market, have an overview of the upcoming season's trends, have designed and sampled your collection, and made sure the production capabilities are in place, it's finally time to sell your product line. The roles you will take on yourself here might differ depending on whether or not you have a retail or wholesale business strategy, but whether you sell your range yourself and control your own PR and marketing in house or use an agent (see Chapter 12), you will need help to create a buzz about you and your line (see Chapter 11). Fashion stylists, photographers, and journalists all help create the necessary awareness of your product and brand that helps drive the sales needed to pump money back into your business. Even though these roles will not be internal to your business you will still need to think about the stories, product, images, and so on that will grab their attention.

Even if you are not going to have your own store, you will need to find a way to educate the retail managers and sales assistants in the stores to which you will wholesale. For many of your customers these third-party representatives will be their first contact with your brand. The more they know about the product and your philosophy, the easier it will be for them to sell your line.

Sales manager:
✖ Manages new and existing accounts
✖ Builds relationships
✖ Sets sales targets
✖ Inputs orders and deals with customer deliveries and returns
✖ Maintains the showroom and books in sales appointments
✖ Selects which exhibitions and promotional fashion shows to take part in
✖ Is responsible for the distribution of samples, price lists, and lookbooks.

Allocator:
✖ Distributes orders to stores, making sure the correct sizes and volumes reach the right stores
✖ Chases suppliers for production
✖ Oversees stock replenishment and reorders.

PR/marketing manager:
✖ Promotes the brand and its products, using advertising, public relations, sales promotion, personal selling, visual merchandising, and the internet
✖ Develops and maintains media relations across fashion stylists, journalists, and editors
✖ Plans and executes company events from fashion shows to photo shoots and press days.

Fashion stylist:
✖ Creates visual looks for catwalk shows and images, such as photographs used in lookbooks, ad campaigns, websites, and fashion editorials.

Stylists play an important role in getting the overall visual presentation of a collection right, whether it be for a catwalk show, lookbook, or advertising campaign

Fashion journalist:
- ✖ Analyzes and/or promotes fashion products
- ✖ Communicates the constantly changing fashion market to the consumer.

Retail manager:
- ✖ Is responsible for the day-to-day running of a store or department, maximizing sales and profit
- ✖ Manages and motivates a team to increase sales and ensure efficiency.

Sales assistant:
- ✖ The "face" of the store, responsible for promoting and selling products direct to customers
- ✖ Liaises with clients (in all areas, client interaction is vital and sales assistants working with higher-priced goods will need to take a very personalized approach).

The key to the success of a one-person operation is to focus on the area you do well in and know when to outsource to trained professionals. Obviously, the more roles you are able to deliver yourself the fewer costs you will incur; however, don't spread yourself too thin. In the long run a little expenditure on staff in the right places can go a very long way.

TASKS

1 *Identify how many of these roles you will undertake yourself. Make a list of those you will need to outsource.*

2 *Research local fashion colleges for potential talent and read ads in fashion trade magazines to get an idea of salaries and freelance wages in your area.*

Hiring and Firing

Being the boss means that you are responsible for appointing the right personnel, managing your team, and firing ineffective staff. Without any managerial experience this can often be a daunting task. Although you may be in a rush with the workload starting to pile up, make sure you take your time finding the right candidates. The worst thing for any small fashion label is to recruit someone who doesn't live up to your expectations. The interview process is your opportunity to make sure you are getting the right person for the job.

Tips for Interviewers

Charlotte Kramer—*Human Resources Specialist and Executive*

THE FOUR P's

Prepared
In advance of the interview, review the candidate's resume and prepare a list of relevant questions.

Professional
You are a representative of your organization, so be prompt to the meeting and professional throughout. Furthermore, consider that while you are deciding whether to hire the candidate, the candidate will be contemplating whether he or she would like to work for you. At the end of the interview process, follow up to let the candidate know the outcome.

Productive
Begin the meeting with a brief outline of the interview process, provide an overview of the organization and the mission. Outline the role, including key responsibilities, objectives, and any team structure. Pose a series of pertinent questions and subsequently encourage the candidate to put questions to you.

Probing
Ask some "open" questions: "Tell me about a time when you..." and "Give me an example of...." Explore past performance, skills, and qualifications. Seek to understand potential weaknesses and areas for greater development: "Tell me about an aspect of your role you wish to improve."

Keep Them Motivated

Once you have the right people you need to keep them motivated. As a start-up fashion business you can't afford to have anyone on the team who is content just to pick up a pay packet. You need your team to be ambitious and as hungry as you are for the business to establish itself. Try to create an environment that means your staff can flourish. This means you need to:

* **Pay attention:** It is all too easy to become bogged down in your own day-to-day activities. Be aware of how your staff are feeling and acting.

* **Implement an appraisal scheme:** Everybody wants feedback on how they are performing. By setting a schedule for constructive feedback you will also have a platform for discussing how you feel your staff are doing. In the first year a one-month, three-month, six-month, and twelve-month review are advisable, with an annual appraisal after that.

* **Offer training and development:** Consider offering further training for staff members to fill any skills gaps or to increase their knowledge base.

* **Create a collaborative and friendly work culture:** In a small, creative business it is important to create the right atmosphere. While some people flourish in a dictatorial environment, most employees need some room to express themselves. Your success will be determined by how productive your staff are and how long they stay working for you. As a start-up fashion label you can't afford a high staff turnover.

Sometimes you will have to let people go. Firing someone can be a horrible experience and can become even worse if you find yourself being sued for unfair dismissal. You must make sure you follow the correct steps when terminating someone's employment.

Things to Think About When Considering Terminating the Employment of an Employee

===

Charlotte Kramer—*Human Resources Specialist and Executive*

----

* *Maintain documentation demonstrating examples of under-performance/ misconduct as well as written records of performance discussions and developmental plans.*
* *Address all possible areas for improvement, such as participation in relevant training and development courses or an appropriate behavioral program.*
* *Adhere to disciplinary policies/local employment legislation.*
* *Consider suitable alternative employment opportunities within the organization.*
* *Treat the employee fairly.*
* *Act with sensitivity and confidentiality.*

===

Case Study: Gil Carvalho

In the fall of 2003, at the age of 27, Portuguese footwear designer Gil Carvalho set up Carvalho Concept Ltd, a high-end luxury ladies' shoe label. He had studied at Cordwainers College, part of the London College of Fashion, graduating with a first class BA in Design, Marketing, and Product Development, and then went on to work for Vivienne Westwood.

After a brief stint with Westwood, Gil realized that his future lay in forming his own company. "The decision to launch my own company was so that I could have total control over my product from concept to production." With the help of some close friends he set about developing his first ready-to-wear collection, along with a conceptual collection to help him reach his ultimate goal—to make the name Gil Carvalho synonymous with luxury.

The first season's collection was entirely self-financed and included a total of 12 styles, each in three color options. Prices ranged from £190 to £1,000. Gil has had a lot of success since he started the label, but it took three years for the company to break even.

Gil believes that patience is important when running a fashion business. He also sees drive and perseverance as two major reasons for his success. He says that "it helps to know your own mind, because everybody involved in fashion has an opinion!"

Understanding his target market was a key factor for Gil in both his sales and manufacturing strategies. "Luxury ladies' shoes are synonymous with Italian production so I felt there was really no choice but to manufacture there." He then decided to target the UK market, but soon became aware of the international appeal of the shoes and started to pursue the US and Italian markets.

Wholesale is an important part of Gil's sales strategy and, although he plans at some stage to open his own retail premises, at this stage he recognizes that it is too early to be considering the expense of a shop. As he is looking to attract an international market he has taken his product to a number of trade shows and, after initial research, narrowed it down to Micam in Milan, WSA in Las Vegas, and Première Classe in Paris. There were more, but these were considered the most

important and met his strict budget demands at the beginning. As the company expands he is looking at involvement in other shows, and his export business now accounts for the largest part of his overall sales.

Gil sees promotion as a key part of the success of a fashion business, valuing it above placement and price. "Never underestimate the effects of good PR; in fashion this is extremely important and cannot be underestimated. PR is fundamental; get this right and the rest follows." However Gil believes that one of the biggest challenges to getting good PR is "market saturation and getting the industry to take notice. All too often the magazines, the main point of reference for the customer, stick to the established brands and give scant regard to new and emerging talent."

In an attempt to break into the established media Gil initially looked to outsource his PR to an agency but very soon decided that the best way forward was to establish his own in-house PR. This allowed him to reduce his outgoings and make sure that the product remained his priority. He has also decided to look at the catwalk as a means of promoting his label but admits it can be difficult as shoes "are seen as the accessory to the main event, which is an obstacle that must be overcome." He believes that product visibility is of the utmost importance and that the catwalk is often one of the best ways to achieve this, allowing you to "showcase a more extreme and conceptual product, which draws attention to your work."

One of the biggest motivations for Gil is "seeing my shoes on the shelves and feeding the shoe-lover's addiction with a must-have design! On a more serious note, the opportunities that present themselves once people begin to appreciate your work are massively important. For me, the recognition of someone established in the industry, and whose work I love, is the ultimate accolade."

In order to reach an international audience, Gil wholesales his shoes through trade shows in London, Las Vegas, Paris, and Milan

*F*ar too many new fashion labels spend the first three to four seasons finding out who their customers are, where they shop, and what is and isn't right for them. The more you know about the market you are about to enter, the more you can be sure about the viability of your product. More importantly, the more research you undertake before you start to put money down on developing your first sample range, the more money you will save in the long run. This chapter will take you through the market research process.

Research Your Market

Market research is all about obtaining and analyzing information in order to make sure you have the right product to deliver to your customer. It also plays a major role in supporting your business plan. Investors or banks will want to know what research you have undertaken to back up your projections. This can be achieved through "secondary" research (information in the press, databases, directories, reports, and books) as well as your own "primary" research (original information obtained through surveys and observation). The latter will be more focused and therefore more useful.

Know Your Customer

You need to know who your customers are. Many young designers develop products at a price point that they themselves could not afford. They often make assumptions about customers and their buying habits. You need to know everything about the types of people who will buy your product if you are to develop a product that meets their needs and wants.

You need to find out about your customers' spending habits, lifestyle, likes and dislikes, and, most importantly, their needs. Knowing why people are buying your product makes it easier to give them the ideal product. Spending time in boutiques and stores, watching how customers shop and what product they pick up and buy can be a great way of getting to know your customer. Working in a retail establishment that you hope to sell to can be invaluable. If you have direct access to people's buying habits and seasonal expenditure you can start to develop your product around this. You will begin to get an idea of what they feel is missing from their wardrobe. Failing this, getting out on the street in a shopping district where your competitors are located and asking passers-by specific questions can give you a pretty good understanding of their buying habits, needs, and wants, and how best to grab their attention.

Fashion hall at Pure London trade show

Profiling Your Target Customer

Demographic	Buying Habits	Likes/Dislikes
Occupation?	Where do they shop?	Favorite designer?
Age?	How do they shop (impulse, sales, seasonally)?	What magazines do they read?
Married, single, divorced?	Are they trend-driven?	What newspaper do they read?
Do they have children?	Are they brand-loyal?	What celebrity do they admire?
Annual income?	What function do they buy for (casual or occasion)?	What is their biggest dislike in fashion?
Where do they live?	How body-conscious are they (enhance or hide)?	What makes them laugh?
Where do they go on vacation?	What is their spending bracket?	What music do they listen to?
How many vacations do they take a year?		
What size do they wear?		

TASK

Create a customer profile
Answer the above questions to create a profile of your ideal customer. Try to create as many different profiles as possible, so that when you market and promote your brand or shop you cover all possible angles. Ask yourself any other questions that you feel might help you better understand your customer.

Having identified your ideal customer, you need to be certain there are enough of them for you to supply. Looking at other fashion labels that offer similar products to yours can give you an indication of this.

Watch Your Competitors

Studying your potential competitors will save you a lot of time and money by using research that others have already undertaken. If similar offers on the market are doing well you can feel confident that a market exists for your product line. First, however, you must decide exactly who your market rivals will be.

By identifying similar labels you can target their current stockist list, knowing that your product will be appreciated. You can also see exactly the types of style, colorway, length, print, trim, and so on that work well for your competitors. Most importantly, you will be able to identify what your customer will expect to pay for certain products, at entry, mid, and top-end price points. If you identify the wrong competitors at the beginning you will waste a lot of time and energy targeting the wrong retailers and customer base. Take your time and get it right.

It is unrealistic to expect retailers and customers to see you in the same light as a superbrand such as Gucci or Ralph Lauren without the history and brand recognition behind you. There are many fashion labels that you may never have heard of but that are doing very good business. A number of your direct competitors probably already exist within this group and you will be able to

Attending trade shows is a great way of researching your competition

gather a lot more information about their activities than about those of any of the big established labels.

Going to trade fairs, identifying similar labels, seeing where they stock (not only shops but countries), and looking at the PR they have achieved will help you to build a business template and develop a better understanding of who will buy your product and why.

Just because you see a label in major fashion publications doesn't mean it is thriving. The fashion industry has a history of PR-friendly labels that have littered the pages of *Vogue*, *Harper's Bazaar*, and *Elle* and are now never heard of. Make sure you do your research properly, identifying labels that have both commercial and press appeal.

===

TASK

Analyze the competition
Choose one competitor already selling in your market and do a SWOT analysis of them (see page 108). Can you exploit any of their weaknesses or threats?

===

Tailor Your Product to Your Market

What will make your product special (see Chapter 9)? Start by identifying your competitors' strengths and weaknesses and see how you can beat their offer.

You need to identify what is already on the market—otherwise you cannot guarantee that you won't just be offering more of the same, but worse, at a higher price. The fashion business is very unforgiving—having the wrong product or price will lead to rejection of your label. Work out how you should tailor your product to meet your customers' needs and how this will give you an edge.

The fashion market is very crowded, with thousands of labels competing worldwide for distribution. You need to have a USP to break into the market and create a viable business. The more time you spend looking at labels that have been on the market for some time, or new ones that are making a splash, the easier it will be for you to determine what it is that makes them successful.

Get the Price Right
The success of your label will also depend on correct pricing for your market. Having studied your competitors' product lines you should have been able to identify a pricing structure. What are their entry (cheapest), mid-range, and high-end (most expensive) price points and what proportion of their range do

Womenswear label Noir has successfully tailored its product to fit into a new and expanding market aimed at combining ethical fashion with designer luxury (see page 20)

they offer at each end of the pricing spectrum (see Chapter 9)? You should also be able to get an understanding of the detailing, finish, and design required to sell the product at that price point. If your competitor is selling a printed silk top for $135 and the product is similar to your product, you can establish that there is a market at that price point for your offer. Just double check that your competitor actually has a successful business. If you log on to their website and find they are stocking in a number of stores, they are probably doing well.

Most customers will have a limit on how much they will pay for a particular product. A designer dress selling at up to $295 may be within their limit, but as soon as you hit the $300 mark a barrier will come down. Luxury shoppers, however, might feel $300 is too inexpensive—the dress is not exclusive enough. By offering the right product at the right price you will promote both customer loyalty and referral and move your fashion label a step closer to becoming a viable business.

However, you should be aware that according to anti-trust law, the rule of thumb is that once you sell your goods to another you surrender any control as to the price they will be re-sold at, or as to where and how they may be distributed. This means that a retailer or distributor can sell your product at a much higher or much lower price than you intended. The only way that you can keep some control over the positioning of your product on the market is by carefully choosing which retailers you supply to, rather than by imposing restrictive covenants on distributors.

Marketing and PR

Marketing and PR will be very important in the development and overall success of your label (see Chapter 12). You need to know which media your potential customer taps into. This includes the newspapers, magazines, and websites they look to for information, as well as the best places to grab their attention with any proposed advertising. Without this insight your advertising and promotional campaigns will be a stab in the dark. Although every designer may want their product to appear in *Vogue,* appearing in *Elle* may do more for your business in reaching your target consumer and turning good PR and advertising into actual sales. If this is the case you should concentrate more of your efforts on developing relationships with the staff at *Elle*. Equally, you may spend a lot of time and energy organizing a catwalk show to promote your label when the money might be better spent on trade exhibitions and press days.

Determine from the outset which media you need to target. You need to know the publications your target customer reads to make sure you are targeting the right one. You can phone the advertising desk of any publication to find out the demographic of their readership. They have this information on hand for potential advertisers who want to make sure they are targeting the right consumer.

Channels of Distribution

How your customer has access to your product will determine how they will view your brand and its image.

Is your business going to be retail, wholesale, or both? Whatever you decide will have a major impact on the financing of your business and on your marketing and PR strategy. Researching how some of your competitors started up and developed their business can be a good starting point for determining your distribution strategy. Websites often give details of a company's history and growth.

You can, once again, look to your competition for an indication of the best outlets for your product. If you are wholesaling, you will want to find out at which exhibitions and showrooms your competitors showcase their collections. National fashion councils and exhibition websites will provide this information. You can also look at your competitors' websites for their lists of current stockists—if a shop has bought their product it may be interested in yours.

Where and how your product is introduced to the consumer is of great importance

If you want to open a retail outlet you may find that by looking your competitors in the eye (setting up your store in the same street or area) you are able to piggyback on their marketing activities and build a customer base from existing passing shoppers. Just make sure that the competition isn't too fierce and the potential share of customers too small.

TASK

Develop a list of potential stockists
Visit stores that you would like to sell to, and identify ten competitors whose product you would like to see yours sitting next to. Visit their websites to view their lists of current stockists. Research the stockists to establish what other brands they sell and then visit the websites of these brands to see if their product complements yours. If it does, look at their stockist lists and continue cross-referencing stockists with brands until you have a sizeable database that you can use for the PR and marketing of your first collection.

Find the Right Location

Location is absolutely fundamental to success if you aim to retail. Spend time deciding where will be the best location for you to set up to maximize your potential to sell: main street, shopping center/mall, freestanding, website, markets, or home shopping parties (see Chapter 11).

Getting the right location for your retail store is vital

Retail Checklist

===

Demographic
Is the area mainly residential or business? Are income levels in this area generally high or low? What is the average shopper like?

Market trend information
How progressive is the community? Does it promote business activity? Is it receptive to change? Are shops open in the evenings or on Sundays? How many businesses opened and closed during the last 12 months? What are the major employers in the community? What is the anticipated growth in the area around the potential site? What are the business trends of the community?

Competition information
Using a map, place an "X" where the competitors are located. Circle the best potential sites. Complete an analysis of each competitor. Are your competitors currently involved in any advertising or promotional activities?

Traffic and accessibility
✖ *Distance from residential areas*	✖ *Public transport*
✖ *Distance from business areas*	✖ *Best side of the street*
✖ *Parking availability*	✖ *Location on street*
✖ *Traffic congestion*	✖ *Appropriate business neighbors*

When does a normal shopping situation occur?
✖ *Day of the week*	✖ *Season*
✖ *Time of day*	✖ *Weather conditions*
✖ *Week of the month*	

Cost considerations
✖ *Rent/mortgage*	✖ *Decorating*
✖ *Business rates*	✖ *Security*
✖ *Utilities*	✖ *Insurance*
✖ *Improvements*	✖ *Other*

Terms of the lease
✖ *Length of lease*	✖ *Option to renew*
✖ *Option to purchase*	✖ *Amount of rent and when payable*
✖ *Description of the space*	✖ *Restrictions on remodeling*
✖ *Restrictions on posting of signs*	✖ *Landlord's responsibilities*
✖ *Insurance requirements*	✖ *Status of tenant if space is sold*
✖ *Sub-letting arrangements*	

===

Additional material for this chapter supplied by Giacomo Corrado, Esq.
Corrado Montgomery, New York

Case Study: Anne Fontaine

Anne Fontaine established her Anne Fontaine womenswear label in Paris in 1993 at the age of 22. Often referred to as "the Queen of the White Shirt", she has seen her business grow rapidly over the past 15 years from her first boutique in Paris in 1994 into an internationally renowned global empire with stores represented in major cities, including New York's Madison Avenue (opened 2000), Shanghai (opened 2005), and Tokyo (opened 2006).

From the very outset Anne and her husband and business partner Ari Zlotkin focused their business around the core concepts of "simplicity, innovation, and independence", and have worked to offer a female customer base "a grand vision of contemporary luxury" that still remains at the heart of their business today. By 2004, sales had risen to €70 million, they employed almost 400 staff, and their product was sold at 65 points of sale in 14 countries worldwide.

Though not having formally studied fashion, Anne's creativity was evident at an early age when she made her own clothes. A journey through the heart of the Amazon rainforest instilled in her a love of natural materials and an understanding of their virtues, and would serve as the basis for the Anne Fontaine brand. It was, however, the chance discovery of an old white shirt that would find Anne imagining "a place where any woman could find such a simple shirt, or blouse, or cache-coeur [crossover top]—the basics of a wardrobe—that would permit her to choose a fashion point of view according to her mood" and would serve as the catalyst for the start of the business.

Anne approached Ari with the idea of designing the very first collection of white shirts entirely for women. Over 500 styles were conceived in that first season from her initial concept, which were then whittled down into a smaller selection to launch the very first Anne Fontaine collection. Anne's experience in the rainforest and her natural sensitivities towards environmental issues had exposed her to the vast array of natural fibers and allowed her to explore within such a simple concept as "the white shirt" a multitude of options to offer her clients.

What started with poplin, piqué cotton, and organdie soon included linen, lace, and many other new natural fabrics that Anne was discovering every season. "The fabrics serve as a source of inspiration not only through their intrinsic form, but also through the particular qualities that temper their feeling upon contact with the skin."

After the choice of fabrics came the development of signature details within her designs: double collars, embroidered flowers, lacing, or vertiges, a word that Anne employs to refer to "highly personal ruching which appears in a variety of different forms in each collection." Ultimately, Anne is looking to offer her customers "allure" and believes this has been the key to her success. With the right cut and a mastery of fabrics she has been able to offer the wearer "a second skin, a familiar and reliable piece of clothing that guarantees a natural and spontaneous elegance that can stem only from the natural sense of breathability that it gives to the woman wearing it."

Comfort and functionality also play a huge part in the objective of Anne's designs and every season she looks for "new approaches to elegance adapted to every personality and every possible mix of occasions." And while new ideas are constantly being developed the process remains the same as when she started, with 500 new designs being put forward for consideration twice a year. "It's still the very same struggle to decide just which ones will make up the 100 select models to be set out for American, Japanese, Chinese, or French customers in the shops of Paris, New York, or Tokyo."

Product and vision remain at the heart of the Anne Fontaine brand, but the virtues of the materials that Anne sees as so essential to the success of her clothing range are not limited to clothing alone and, taking inspiration from her Amazonian experiences, she has developed the Anne Fontaine Spa, where she is able to share her experience of "the therapeutic virtues of these natural treasures. Cotton, silk, and wild bamboo are at the heart of the signature treatments at Spa Anne Fontaine, and lay the grounds for its exclusivity."

Twelve years after opening the first Anne Fontaine Boutique in Paris, the new location on Rue Saint-Honoré was opened in 2006, allowing Anne, for the first time, to present her complete vision for the brand by uniting a boutique and spa.

The Anne Fontaine boutique on Rue Saint-Honoré, Paris, was opened in 2006. The boutique allows Anne for the first time to deliver her complete concept for the brand with the Anne Fontaine Spa and her trademark white shirts under one roof

ANNE FONTAINE

Chapter 8: Understanding Trends

*T*rends play an important role in the world of fashion; you must understand how they work and how you can use them to your best advantage. You will have to decide how focused on trends your particular customer base is. Your initial research should have given you a good understanding of your potential customer and you should be able to determine whether your shopper is trend-driven. You should develop your product accordingly. Your product success will be determined by your ability to meet the needs of your customers. This chapter will show you how to find out what your customers actually want and how they are influenced by trends.

What Is a Fashion Trend?

A "fashion trend" can be defined as the movement of fashion over a period of time. What is in fashion one season may be out the next. Fashion trends are all about the "latest" or the "newest." In recent years, "new" has tended to mean that the product has been missing or scarce in the marketplace for a while and is being reintroduced by designers or retailers. It may only be truly new to the generation of consumers who missed the trend the first time around.

Trends do not have to be seasonal. The 1990s saw the start of a trend for more casual dressing in the workplace that still can be seen today.

Other trends burst into the stores, are worn for a very limited time, then disappear just as quickly as they emerged. These varying lifespans of trends are known as "fashion cycles." A trend's fashion cycle is determined by the number of people (adopters) that buy into the look and how long it takes for the look to take off and eventually die out. In order for something to become fashionable it has to be accepted by the consumer. Although a designer or retailer may push a particular style, if it is not bought and worn there is no trend.

Different Categories of Trend
Within the fashion cycle itself we can identify different categories of trends by looking at the lifespan of the trend as well as the speed of the rise and decline of the adoption period. Some of the key differences within the cycle include:

Classics
A fashion look that has been around longer than expected. Retailers sell classics season after season. Examples include the white shirt, the trench coat, and the little black dress (LBD). The style never completely dies.

Tokyo street style

Fads

Fads are those products that have a very short shelf-life, arriving on the scene with a big splash, only to disappear just as quickly. Although fads have a short lifecycle, clever designers and retailers are able to capitalize on fads to keep customers and the press interested.

Cycles within cycles

Successful designers are able to tinker with design elements (such as color, texture, or silhouette) to offer "newness" to a popular product, keeping it fresh and maximizing its lifespan. A great example of this is, again, the LBD, which has become a staple of any fashionista's wardrobe. It is always being updated.

Fashions are classified as a classic or a fad by looking at how quickly they progress through the six phases of the fashion lifecycle (see below). A fad may go through all six stages within one season, whereas a classic may never reach stage six, declining only for a while before being reintroduced.

Fashion Lifecycle Phases

==

1 **Innovation:** *Fashion leaders will pay high prices for new looks.*
2 **Rise:** *More people start to adopt the key looks.*
3 **Acceleration:** *The look is copied by many retailers and adopted by fashion followers.*
4 **General acceptance:** *The look reaches its maximum sales potential and is to be seen everywhere.*
5 **Decline:** *Sales decline as new trends emerge; retailers reduce prices and start to replace the look with a newer trend.*
6 **Obsolescence:** *The look is no longer to be seen.*

==

The LBD, or little black dress,
is a classic that is constantly
revisited and often updated
by designers

Who Leads and Who Follows Fashion

It is the fashion leaders who drive new looks forward, but a trend truly relies on the fashion followers to legitimize it.

Diffusion of Innovation

In 1962 Everett Rogers formulated his "diffusion of innovations" theory in his book, *Diffusion of Innovations*. He argued that adopters of any new innovation or idea could be categorized as innovators (2.5%), early adopters (13.5%), early majority (34%), late majority (34%), and laggards (16%). He argued that the willingness and ability of each group to adopt an innovation would depend on their awareness, interest, evaluation, and trial. Although this theory can sometimes be over-simplistic, it goes a long way towards defining the key attributes and reasons behind trend adoption. Here are some of the key characteristics defining each group:

Fashion innovators

These are the earliest communicators of a new style or look to other fashion consumers. They may or may not be influential in making other people like the style, but they create the awareness and provide the visual display and initial exposure of the style. They feel more socially secure and are more interested in fashion than others.

Early adopters

Early adopters legitimize a style for fashion followers. They influence people in their social group but stay within the social norms of the group. They may also adopt a slightly modified or toned-down version of a style after innovators have received attention from others. Early adopters are crucial for the mainstreaming of trends.

Early majority

The early majority are very deliberate in their purchases and look to those more stylish for guidance. They are influenced by advertising and media but are more driven to look good for the sake of fitting in with those around them.

Late majority

The late majority are more skeptical of the "latest" or "newest" fashions and will take time to be convinced. However, they want to be considered part of the group and will therefore follow the herd. They tend to have more traditional tastes and quite often come from lower socio-economic backgrounds.

Laggards

Laggards look to neighbors and friends. They are looking for comfort and ease of wear and are not interested in trends. They also have a fear of debt and are therefore the least likely to impulse-buy.

We tend to define those in the first two groups as "change agents" or "innovative communicators"—those people that help to move fashion forward. Those in the remaining groups are "fashion followers," and tend to look to others for guidance.

When plotted on a graph, Rogers' theory of diffusion looks as below.

A market exists at each of these stages, with the consumers in the biggest market segments being considered fashion followers. You will therefore need to decide in which segment your ideal customer sits and develop your product line accordingly.

Rogers also proposed a five-stage model for the diffusion of innovation. He argued that adopters would go through each stage before ultimately deciding whether or not to accept the innovation.

1 **Knowledge:** Learning about the existence and function of the innovation.

2 **Persuasion:** Becoming convinced of the value of the innovation.

3 **Decision:** Committing to the adoption of the innovation.

4 **Implementation:** Putting the innovation to use.

5 **Confirmation:** The ultimate acceptance (or rejection) of the innovation.

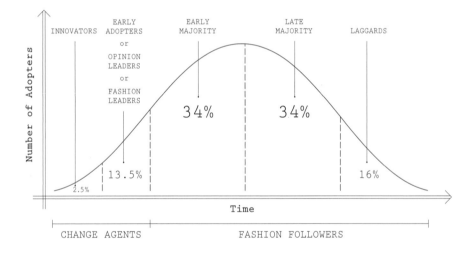

If you consider yourself an innovative designer and are hoping to develop new trends, your marketing and PR will have to work hard to get the customer to work through these five stages. Many great young designers don't even get enough exposure to let the consumer know their product exists, let alone give them the chance to buy it and offer confirmation of the look. The catwalk is usually the place for this type of design and you will need to target the fashion press to gain the initial recognition you will require.

Characteristics of Innovators v Early Adopters/Mainstream

Innovators	Early Adopter/Mainstream
Creative	Want entertainment, to consume
Participators	Spectators; just read about it
Risk-takers	Want comfort, to fit in
Create own identity	Ease of mass market and media definition
Unusual level of passion	Want safety, to fit in, to go where the herd goes
Interested in change/novelty	Like comfort and stability, don't think too much

High Fashion v Mass Fashion

✖ *High-fashion looks are created by designers and exclusive stores.*
✖ *Fashion leaders buy these looks during the introduction and growth stages.*
✖ *The goods are expensive but exclusivity is what fashion leaders crave.*

✖ *Mass fashion is made by manufacturers and retailers at many price points.*
✖ *Fashion followers wear mass fashion.*
✖ *Fashion laggards want good value; they buy late.*

What Influences Fashion Trends?

Several factors influence fashion trends from season to season and from decade to decade. These can include: technology, economic conditions, social conditions, media, celebrities, and peer groups.

Designers are influenced by their surroundings and current events. Moods and feelings play an important part in the development of designs and different designers are often influenced by the same factors—this can be seen in their designs. In times of uncertainty it is common to see more structure and tailoring in muted colors on the catwalks. When things begin to pick up you may see vibrant colors combined with fluid tailoring and fabrics.

Trends may develop along a safe and predictable route—from a previous season's product or as a reaction against a trend that has become saturated. Designers and retailers can also be cautious about introducing a trend. They may introduce some product into their stores to test their customers' reactions before putting their money into a big production run. This is known as a "trial balloon." If the product is not well received it will disappear from the store and not become a trend.

Before committing large amounts of their budget, retailers will often see how customers react to a new trend by trialing the product in-store

Theories of Fashion Leadership

Several theories have been developed about how fashion spreads:

"Trickle down" theory

Fashion spreads from the top down. At the top are the fashion icons and style gurus. The retail chains and the consumer watch what is happening on the catwalks or being worn by the celebrities and interpret the trends to fit into their market or lifestyle.

Celebrities (David Beckham, Emma Watson) and royal figures (Kate Middleton, now Duchess of Cambridge) can become fashion icons, legitimizing a look for the general public and having a huge influence on sales. This is one of the reasons why so many designers try so hard to get their product on an A-lister's back. A single picture of the right celebrity can be syndicated worldwide, giving your product and label instant global exposure (see Chapter 12).

"Trickle across" theory

Fashion spreads horizontally within and across groups. Each segment of society will have its own leaders to whom it will look for guidance on what is and isn't acceptable. This can range from a young executive looking to the boss for behavioral and dress guidelines, to a group of friends, of whom one is a trendsetter. Most of us want to fit in, so we won't be the first to adopt a new look and will require affirmation of the trend from others around us. However, we don't want to be the last to adopt the look as we will then look out of place. Ultimately, our need to fit in dictates our adoption of certain trends.

"Trickle up" theory

Trends that have their origins within sub-groups of society will often find their way upwards into the mainstream. Both the retail chains and high-end designers will often look to street culture for their inspiration. Think of how the fashions of US hip-hop culture have gone mainstream in retailers all over the world, and have even found their way on to the catwalks of London, Paris, New York, and Milan.

Trends may trickle down, across, and up to reach their target customer. The more tuned in you are to what is taking place on the catwalks, on the streets, and among your own friends, the easier it will be to identify potential trends. Many designers don't go out of their way to predict a trend, but their ongoing search for inspiration often means they are on-trend season after season.

Media Influences on Trends

The media plays a very important role in influencing what is and isn't on-trend. Designers and retailers create themes within a seasonal collection, with a selection of looks that will appeal to as broad a range of buyers as possible. Themes across different designer collections tend to happen because designers and fabric manufacturers have to predict so far ahead that they work to a creative formula. By studying previous trends and the current mood and environment designers can predict, albeit often subconsciously, where the market is progressing or even returning to.

Fashion writers, who see hundreds of fashion shows and lookbooks each season, will group the work of the designers in order to write about it in a way their readers can understand. This means looking at key pieces and themes that stick out in enough of the collections to get their attention. Buyers from boutiques and department stores also take note of the trends and work out which will appeal to their customers. Customers read about what's hot and what's not—when the new looks and trends appear in the fashion press a demand is created, and the boutiques and department stores are then ready to sell the garments that have been praised and singled out.

 ## How Trend-Driven Should You Be?

This depends on the customer you aim to target. You may decide that being a slave to the trends would actually be detrimental to your business, and focus more on developing a distinctive identity that your customer will want season after season (see Chapter 9).

It is difficult to compete with the bigger labels and retail chains in the trend stakes. Retail chains will have a number of different trends each season, safe in the knowledge that if one doesn't take off as well as they hoped they have others the consumer can buy into. If you have put all your eggs in one basket and then discover that the look for the season isn't the one you decided on, the effect on your sales will be devastating.

However, cleverly introducing elements of trends into your collection—color, fabric, sizing, and styling—while not taking away the essence of who and what your label is, can help to move your product forward. Being on-trend can also help in attracting the attention of fashion magazines that need to show their readers the latest looks.

You could try to allocate a percentage of your collection each season to experiment with trend-led ideas. This will give you the freedom to create new and exciting ideas while focusing the rest of the collection on your already established, tried-and-true designs.

You may also find, depending on where your customer sits on the diffusion curve (see page 93), that being off-trend is more beneficial to your sales. This is because mainstreamers won't necessarily buy into a new trend straight away and may take another season or two to feel confident that it is right for them. Even when they do buy into the look it is usually a watered-down version. It is therefore imperative to understand the expectations of your customer and develop your product accordingly.

High-end designers are often instrumental in setting the trends for the upcoming seasons, and if this is where you hope your label will sit then you will need to be true to your own vision rather than following others. You will need

When developing a collection, designers will often introduce elements of trend relevant to each season (vest, oversized shirt, skinny trousers) while still offering their more classic pieces (wrap dress)

to work hard at convincing both the press and consumers that your vision is worth their attention. Once you have achieved this you will find that you are being watched for tips for next season. Until this happens, you may be developing innovative designs that nobody wants to wear.

Decide from the start where you believe your customer sits in the trend stakes and look at your competitors to see how trend-driven they really are. You may find that both place more importance on good, well thought-out design.

Legal Protection for your Designs

A new proposed legislation, the Innovative Design Protection and Piracy Prevention Act, which is likely to become effective in the near future, will protect original (unique, novel) designs from any "substantially identical" copy, a protection not yet afforded to fashion houses in the US. Under this new law, original designs would enjoy protection from unlicensed copies (knock-offs infringing upon the original design) for a period of three years since they are introduced into commerce, without any need for registration of the designs or other formality. Opponents of this Act fear that if interpreted narrowly, the proposed law would fail to curb knock-offs which have been sufficiently tweaked and revised to elude the scope of protection. On the other hand, if applied more liberally it may have a chilling effect hindering fashion trends, a vital phenomenon to fashion which naturally requires a degree of copying in order to spread. Finally, the Act carves out an interesting exception ("Home Sewing Exception"), which excludes from the reach of this Act copies made for personal use (as the copy one would ask a tailor to reproduce slavishly from a suit or dress designed by a fashion house).

Additional material for this chapter supplied by Giacomo Corrado, Esq.
Corrado Montgomery, New York

Case Study: Schumacher

In 1989, 24-year-old Dorothee Schumacher established Schumacher in Germany. The label, which started off with five special pieces, has grown into an internationally recognizable brand synonymous with high-quality, sophisticated, yet contemporary pieces for women. Prices range from €89 for a basic shirt, to €449 for dresses and up to €1,200 for a key collection piece. The label began by presenting its key pieces at the Collection Première Düsseldorf, one of the world's most important fashion fairs. After initial success in Germany, interest in the label grew in Switzerland and Austria, almost immediately followed by global success. Today, Schumacher is available in 46 countries and within 600 retailers, with stores full of fantasy and attention to detail. These can be found in cosmopolitan cities like Kuwait, Moscow, Warsaw, and Berlin. Schumacher launched its online store at *www.dorothee-schumacher.com* in September 2010, where the collection is presented in the same atmosphere that the customers will find in the stores. Schumacher has remained a family-run business.

From a very early age Dorothee knew what she wanted to achieve. Fascinated by the flair that surrounds the fashion industry, she went to Italy and France to study textiles. She worked with a number of well-known brands, constantly watching, learning, and developing her own unique style that would serve as the building blocks for the launch of her own label.

From the beginning the product has always come first for Dorothee, who started by designing a shirt that "was different from any other—smart, feminine, and powerful." Dorothee believes "the Schumacher woman relies on her feminine charm as opposed to emulating the male way of dressing," and that it has been this understanding of her customers' needs, combined with her own sense of creativity, that led to the immediate success of her first and subsequent collections. Dorothee feels that it is important for any new label to have "a very strong sense of style and intuitive feel for forthcoming trends, confidence, and conviction, not to mention the perfect balance between the customer's needs and not compromising one's own ideas." Having started with only five pieces, the Schumacher collection now offers a complete range, including coats, dresses, knitwear, shirts, and accessories.

To ensure that the large product range stands up to the scrutiny that Dorothee herself places on each piece, huge importance is placed on the manufacturing process and where the product is made: "In the early years, manufacturing was done exclusively in Italy and Germany, but by 1996–97 Schumacher began to identify countries with the highest level of knowhow in specific fields—embroidery in India, cashmere in Italy, and lace in France—thus guaranteeing the highest quality at all times." This ensures that "the product remains at the heart of our strategy and symbolizes the philosophy and authenticity of Schumacher."

While getting the price right is obviously an important factor in the development of a label, Dorothee says it is not the most important one. "When a customer finds 'the piece,' they are always willing to pay for it," and, as a result, she ranks price behind product and placement. The promotion of the label is developed through an extensive marketing strategy that focuses on the heart of the Schumacher brand. "All our packages, giveaways, and store essentials are unique. The customer does not just buy a piece, but a complete look and the philosophy surrounding it. Schumacher works on word-of-mouth recommendation, therefore our policy is strictly against advertising and licensing." They maintain their PR department in house at their headquarters but work closely with external agencies for international PR.

While Dorothee recognizes there can be disappointments when running your own fashion label she says that "one needs to be positive and always look forward." Her constant motivation comes from "the people surrounding me; the permanent change and regeneration of Schumacher and everything it stands for. I am always eager to learn and having my own brand gives me the opportunity to do this on a day-to-day basis. It is exciting to grow and to enter new arenas." She views Schumacher as a great platform for all her creative thoughts at the same time as enabling her to be a businesswoman. It also allows her to structure her life the way she wants. "By being able to bring my dreams to life I gain a lot of strength. Schumacher also gives me the opportunity to organize my time the way it is best for me and my family."

From an initial collection of just five pieces, Dorothee Schumacher has grown her label into an international brand, which she operates from her headquarters in Germany

*D*eveloping your own product is your chance to express yourself creatively and produce something you feel good about—probably the reason you started on this journey. But it is even more important to ensure that you have a strong profile and a good customer rating. This chapter will outline the rules for making sure that the line you develop creates the impact you need.

Understand Your Customer

If you are serious about developing a clothing line that will allow you to create a lasting business, you must do your market research and have a full understanding of your target customer's lifestyle. Without an understanding of your customer base it is very difficult to determine not only what they will wear but on what occasion they will wear it.

Small start-up fashion labels can often be self-indulgent, designing with themselves in mind, in the blind self-belief that "I just know other people will love it!" Although this can be good if your taste reflects that of the markets and you fit the profile of your target customer, it is usually a fast-track to failure.

Many young designers starting out do not have the lifestyle, let alone the bank balance, of their target customer and are not designer shoppers themselves. This means that they often make assumptions about the people they hope to sell to, and their product often fails to meet the needs of the consumer.

You need to identify your competitors, analyze what does and doesn't sell for them, determine what your prospective customer is likely to buy and refine your product range accordingly (see Chapter 7).

Getting It Right

If you are going to make your mark, you need to cover all the angles.

Direction and Mood
"Direction" and "mood" are the intangible design elements that are often the difference between success and failure. If you can create a collection that has an immediate message and attitude, and that resonates with your buyer instantly, you have a good chance of selling your product.

You must try to conjure up a mood and spirit that says "this is what my label is about." Just one look should tell your buyer whether your label is feminine, edgy,

Men's tailoring department at Harrods

sophisticated. or sporty. Your marketing materials—lookbooks, websites, catwalk shows—should reinforce the message of your product.

Clare Watson, freelance stylist, says:

"When labels are starting out, I particularly like seeing small collections that are well thought-out and very together, as they are the ones that leave a lasting impression. Time after time, I see new designers who attempt to do a bit of everything to cover all areas, which leaves everyone feeling confused about their style. Once you have established yourself with a style, then is the time to add new ideas that will then be far more easily accepted."

Individuality
Try to create a USP (unique selling point) that allows you to stand out from the crowd and gives buyers a reason to buy you. It sounds easy, but with so much competition it can be hard to be different yet still sellable. Exclusive fabrics, unique cuts, specialized trimmings, bold use of color, and selling price are all examples of ways to distinguish your product, and designing for a niche market can often be a way of ensuring that something is unique.

Commerciality
You want buyers to buy your product for their store and consumers to buy from the store to ensure reorders. Most shops will want to have sold 70 percent of your stock before sale season comes around. (This is called the "sell-through rate" and is always expressed as a percentage. "Net sales" refers to the same thing, in absolute numbers. A low sell-through rate is one factor that may determine whether a store stops buying your product line. You may be given a couple of seasons to improve sales and educate customers about your label, but most buyers will not want to give up valuable rail space to a line that does not bring a good return.) You need to know what is and isn't commercially viable for your market and incorporate this into your product. Good research can help. Once you start to build your stockist list you will get feedback from buyers about what their customers think, with ideas for adjusting your product to increase the potential for sales. It can be quite a challenge to create something both unique and sellable, but this is what successful fashion labels do.

Kat and Oz Aalam, of London boutique Damsel, say:

"[We] offer something different style-wise and take into account how practical our clients are. Dry-clean-only tops for the daytime don't work for us as most of our clients have kids. You also cannot underestimate the WOW factor. People will find a way to pay for something they absolutely love so it's got to be different and grab their attention! The high street's [retail chains'] offer is now so competitive that boutiques like ours find it harder and harder to compete on price. We need to offer something to our customer that they can't get on the high street for a third of the cost.

"Price points are also important—while my sister and I appreciate why beadwork, fabrics, and design features justify high prices, we also know that we probably can't sell tops over £170 [$260] or dresses over £300 [$460]. That's just our market."

Fashion accessories label Knomo was one of the first UK brands to introduce designer laptop bags into the market, instantly giving itself a unique selling point

Quality

A good brand image is all about creating good feeling between yourself and your customer base, especially at the higher price points. It doesn't matter how great your samples looked and how many orders you have taken—if your quality is poor you will fail.

Customers won't buy your product if poor workmanship means the clothes look bad, and they won't buy your product again if quality becomes an issue after purchase. You need to spend as much time getting this right as you do on the design (see Chapter 10).

Value for Money

It doesn't matter how much you are charging for your product—people love to feel they are getting something special. Whether it is a bargain at the price or a bit of pure indulgence and luxury, you need to make your customer feel that they got a really good deal.

Expensive purchases can lead to "cognitive dissonance"—a fear that you haven't made the right decision. You can combat this with product that offers fantastic design, quality, price, and a USP. Marketing and PR play a major role at

Designers like Caroline Charles work hard to maintain a consistent message throughout their collections so that their customers can recognize the designer's handwriting season after season

this point. The more your customers see your label in the press, the more they will be reassured that they have made the right purchase (see Chapter 12).

Consistency and Development

Having worked hard to develop a signature, you must maintain the identity of your label across the seasons, offering a consistent product range from which the buyers can select. Areas for key consideration in maintaining consistency include: design, fit, fabric, and use of color, with a strong emphasis on quality and price. There is nothing worse for a buyer who picks up your label one season than to find that you have completely changed the offer for the following season.

However, you still need to develop your collection from season to season, depending on how the market and trends are moving. Small boutique buyers know that their customer base is limited and, as a result, may be able to sell only so many of a given style. If you are offering the same style season after season there may soon be few customers to buy it. You need to be aware of the trends and how these can be adapted to key sellers within a range, moving the collection on and keeping it fresh, while keeping your signature recognizable.

Balance and Choice

How will your final collection look sitting on a rail in a store? Will it make sense to the customer? Does it have hanger appeal? You need to make sure that you create a balanced collection with enough width and depth or, alternatively, a single product with a strong identity. All the styles in a collection must work together to create a story and provide understandable options to the buyer.

Range Planning

Building a balanced range requires good planning, which will deliver the right amount of choice and quantity within each collection. It combines your design budget and design/selling strategy to create a shopping list for the store buyer. It's about product selection and turning individual products into a commercially viable sample range. It is a key stage in the development of your collection.

The Range Width

The number of different styles/shapes you are going to offer will depend on your selling strategy, price point, and type of product. The more styles you have on offer the greater the choice for the buyer, but it may be wise to limit the number of options you offer initially so as to keep costs to a minimum. You can sometimes deliver greater choice if you limit your product categories. You might decide to specialize in dresses and offer a choice of ten different styles, or you might want a denim range that initially focuses on six different cuts of jean. This not only gives you a choice within a product category but immediately gives you a signature that a buyer can easily recognize.

If, however, you want to create a full range, you may find your number of styles increasing rapidly. Remember that each style added means another pattern to be cut, with an increase in cost and more minimums to meet when it comes to the production run (see Chapter 10).

Schumacher started out with five key pieces and Karen Walker with just one.

The Range Depth

You can produce every style in its own unique fabric, print, or colorway. However, for a start-up label, this can often lead to difficulties in meeting the minimum order requirements of your fabric suppliers. Every style you develop will need to sell well on its own to ensure that you will be able to go into production with it. Too much variation in fabric and color can also make your collection look disjointed and confuse the buyer.

When developing your collection you need to consider "hanger appeal." In other words, how your collection will look when sitting together en masse

By using the same color and fabric options across a number of styles you can create "stories" within your range, making it easier for buyers to comprehend and for you to meet your minimums.

The Price Architecture

Your market research should have given you a good starting point to work out the price that you can sell your product for. Remember that you will usually sell more of your lower-priced goods and your sample range should reflect this by offering a larger selection of pieces at the lower prices and fewer as the price increases. For instance, a basic camisole might be offered in four or five colorways, while a more elaborate party dress might come in just one or two.

Make a Template

Before you start the actual illustrative design process, sit down and work out a template. This should include the total number of pieces you are going to sample with a breakdown of styles, fabric, and color options as well as price points. Although you may have plenty of time with your first collection to get everything the way you want it, you will quickly find that once you are selling and overseeing the production, delivery, and day-to-day running of a business, design time will be limited. A good template can help focus your designing and save time in the long run. It can also be a quick check to see how balanced your range is before you start spending on developing your samples.

Ultimately, good range planning is about predicting what your stockists will buy from you and the price point they will expect. It is about developing a range that is well balanced in color, fabric, and price, cohesive in its number of options— tops or bottoms—and offers a strong statement when hung in a store.

Remember, sometimes less is more. In the template below there is a varied offer of product, but imagine how much choice of dresses there could have been if the 35-piece range only offered dresses and not the complete look. In the case of Anne Fontaine (see page 86) she has narrowed her product range considerably and so delivers greater choice within her categories. It is all about delivering a minimum credible offer to your buyer or consumer.

It is an ongoing exercise and you should analyze sales on a product-by-product basis season after season. It may well take a few seasons for you to work out exactly what your ideal range should be, but the sooner you do so the less money you will waste, the more stockists you will pick up, and the greater your chance of success.

Style Name	Rose print silk crêpe	Black silk crêpe	Red silk crêpe	Polka-dot print silk chiffon	Tulip print cotton	White cotton	Summer blue cotton	Cashmere cream knit	Cashmere black knit	Totals	Price MSRP $
Mini cocktail dress	X	X		X						3	145.00
Maxi dress	X		X	X						3	190.00
Summer dress					X	X	X			3	95.00
Shirt dress						X	X			2	85.00
Backless cami	X	X		X						3	80.00
Party cami		X	X							2	95.00
Tunic	X		X	X						3	110.00
Buttoned-up shirt					X	X	X			3	65.00
Halter top		X		X						2	75.00
Summer knit								X	X	2	130.00
Summer short						X	X			2	45.00
Skinny pant					X		X			2	75.00
Wrap skirt	X		X							2	110.00
Scarf	X			X	X					3	30.00
Totals	6	4	4	6	4	4	5	1	1	35	

When developing your subsequent collections it is important to analyze what has and hasn't worked from the previous season. One way to do this is to undertake a SWOT analysis.

SWOT Analysis

Strengths: What has worked well in the season? Why?
Weaknesses: What hasn't worked well in the season? Why?
Opportunities: What can you do to improve the performance of your label? How can you turn your weaknesses into strengths?
Threats: What outside factors could threaten your label?

Function, Fashionability, and Added Value

Product developers often look at the overall impact a product will have on their chosen market by focusing on the three key areas of function, fashionability, and added value. These can also be helpful for any small fashion label to think about and measure their product range against.

Function

Determine from the start what function your product will serve. People buy clothes for a purpose and by meeting the needs of the customer you are more likely to sell greater numbers. Therefore, if you are developing a range of winter coats, will they be warm? If you are developing swimwear for the beach, will it protect the modesty of the wearer when wet? And, most importantly, will your product make your customers feel confident and good about themselves?

Fashionability

Depending on how fashion-conscious your target customer is and where they fit in the trend hierarchy you will need to pitch the styling, shape, color, fabric, print, and trims of your product accordingly. It is sometimes easier to be a bit behind the trends when developing your range, as you can see what the fashion leaders have already developed and tweak your range to suit (see Chapter 11).

Added Value

This may come from the product itself through the use of unique fabrics, superb fit, and exquisite trims as well as the unexpected—a printed pocket lining; a matching purse within a clutch bag. However, added value can also come from the profile of the designer or brand and the customer's perception of you. Press and advertising will help to develop your label's profile, increasing the added value placed on buying one of your pieces. Do not underestimate the added value of great design.

Customer Impact Diagram

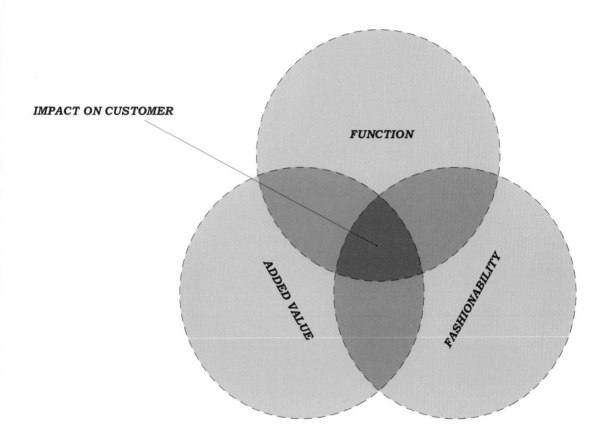

IMPACT ON CUSTOMER

FUNCTION

ADDED VALUE

FASHIONABILITY

===

TASK

Develop your own product-range template

Start off by determining the function of your product and your customer's profile. Then limit yourself to a number of pieces in your collection (20 to 30 may be a good starting point for this exercise) before moving on to decide on styles and colorways. Add rough guideline retail price points. Look back over your template to see if you have balanced the range. Have you used each colorway enough times and are there options for each style? Does your price architecture work?

===

Case Study: Odel

Otara Gunawardene is the founder and CEO of Sri Lanka's pioneering fashion retail chain Odel. The company's flagship store in Colombo is positioned as the Sri Lankan equivalent of Harrods in London and C.K. Tangs in Singapore—it is "not just a department store but also a tourist destination." This complex is the only department store in Sri Lanka, spanning 33,000 square feet (3,100 m^2) and is one of 13 Odel retail outlets around Colombo, with more outlets in the pipeline.

In August 2010 Odel went public at a valuation of US$18 million. Less than six months later the company's share price valued Odel in excess of US$40 million, with Otara still retaining 56 percent ownership. This is all a long way from the humble beginning of the company—Otara came to an arrangement with a friend who ran a factory producing goods for overseas markets, taking some of the excess dead stock that nobody wanted and selling it on to friends for a commission. Anything that didn't sell would go back to the manufacturer. Armed with a box full of old stock and her station wagon Otara drove around Colombo selling out of the trunk of her car. This was in the late 1980s and what Otara was offering in Sri Lanka was fairly radical at the time. As a result she began to garner a reputation and her customer list grew. After over a year of trading out of her car Otara was offered a 500 square foot (46 m^2) space in a three-story building her father owned. The first Odel store was born. At the same time Otara had started making some money out of creating promotional T-shirts for local companies. With this design experience behind her Otara decided to add a range of her own T-shirts promoting the local wildlife, donating funds from the sales to the Wildlife Trust. The store became a success and gradually Otara took over the rest of the building.

Between 1991 and 1994 Otara opened a further nine stores, the majority of which were leased properties, taking out loans with a six- to ten-year repayment option to get the stores up and running. As the business grew Otara started to pay for advertising in tourist board magazines and large roadside billboards, as well as in-store promotions and visual merchandising to attract repeat customers. In 1994 Otara needed a bigger retail space and so took on the Old Colonial Town Hall building that now serves as her flagship department store. With a bigger space Otara needed to bring in more stock, but "surplus was becoming harder to find as others had started to follow suit setting up off-price retailers with end of line surplus," so to differentiate herself from the rest Otara started to focus on developing her own label products. Now the product mix of Odel contains more than 1,500 different items with the majority sourced locally. Odel also sells some international brands but a major reason behind local sourcing has been the fact that often "duties are too high to bring international brands into Sri Lanka and the customer can't afford the price." Today about 40–50 percent of the product on offer is own brand, a percentage that will more than likely increase over the coming years. Own brands include a collection in aid of Embark, an organization established to protect and house Sri Lanka's street dogs—a cause that is very close to Otara's heart.

In the early days there was an initial staff base of just two and Otara relied heavily on help from her family, including her sister-in-law who was an accountant. Now Odel employs more than 430 people directly and a further 500 indirectly. It hasn't all been plain sailing though and Otara hasn't been afraid to learn from her failings. An unsuccessful venture opening a store in Singapore prompted her to study the financial aspects of the business in more detail.

Otara believes that determination and having a point of difference have played a major part in her success so far. "I don't think I'll ever stop dreaming and developing new concepts. I'm planning to look at areas for new stores, improve the current stores, and also look into expanding overseas in the near future." Networking, PR, and marketing have been essential to the business and Otara has been a pioneer in this area within Sri Lanka with the development of her award-winning websites and her use of social media to promote her brands. She also believes that it is imperative for start-ups "to understand the market you are selling to, try to be different, hard-working, and above all enjoy what you do."

Otara has grown Odel from a surplus stock retailer selling from the trunk of her car into a chain of stores selling own-brand fashion and lifestyle products with a value of over $40 million

Chapter 10: Getting it Made

*H*ow and where to get your product made is often the most daunting part of setting up your own fashion label. Simply put, finding a manufacturer to make the product to the quality and quantity you require and at a price that makes your business plan profitable can be tough. This chapter will introduce you to the process.

Manufacturing Options

It is important to understand the technicalities of the manufacturing process so that you will then be in a better position to make the decision that best suits your product and overall supply chain. Your manufacturing options include:

In House:
✖ Common for fashion start-ups where the designer is technically trained in pattern cutting and machining
✖ Allows for very small quantities to be developed
✖ You keep close control over quality
✖ Can be problematic when larger orders have to be produced
✖ You are responsible for sourcing all of the components.

Cottage Industry:
✖ Outsources the sampling/production of your product to technically proficient skilled labor (pattern cutters/seamstresses), usually working from home
✖ Can be charged by the hour, by the day, or by the pattern/garment/accessory
✖ Allows very small numbers of each style to be developed
✖ If sourced locally, you can maintain close control over the quality
✖ Can be problematic when larger orders have to be produced
✖ You are responsible for sourcing all of the components.

CMT (Cut, Make, Trim):
✖ Outsources sampling/production to a production unit with a number of technical workers who will cut, make, and add trims
✖ Allows for smaller production runs and more potential for larger runs where needed
✖ You are responsible for sourcing all of the components.

Full Package Manufacturers:
✖ Outsources sampling/production of product to a factory that will give you a fully costed product including patterns, fabrics, and CMT
✖ May provide sourcing services for fabrics and trims as well as developing garment labels/swing tickets

Threads. Image by David Hardy

* Product is delivered to you ready to be shipped to customers
* Depending on the size of the factory it usually allows for greater numbers to be produced.

Production Process

It is quite common for small fashion labels to undertake all of the sampling and production of their garments in house or to rely on small local cottage industries. However, as and when your business grows, it is more than likely that you will need to look at either a Cut, Make, Trim facility or a bigger manufacturing option to meet your demands.

Like everything when you're a start-up it is at the beginning of your journey that the production process is at its hardest. While you may not meet the minimum order quantity stipulated by the bigger manufacturing options in the beginning, and therefore not be able to work with them from the outset, there is no doubt that the full package service they provide will significantly reduce your workload. They will often have established relationships with fabric and trim suppliers that can cut down the costs, minimums, and lead times that you may face as an individual. When you keep production in house or work with a cottage industry or CMT you are directly responsible for sourcing all of the components that go into your product. Depending on how complicated your product is, and how hard-to-find the components that go into making it are, this could mean a great deal of your time spent liaising and sourcing with suppliers and negotiating lead times. It is imperative you remain on top of all of this and this is why the role of Production Manager will be one of the most important that you may

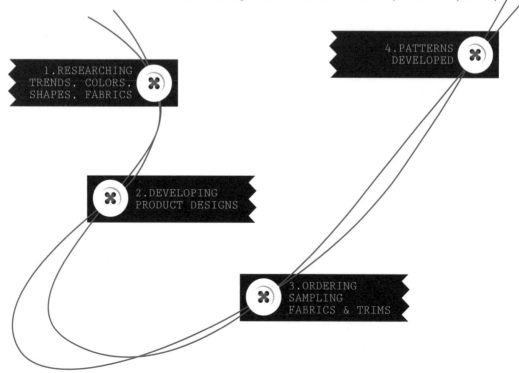

1. RESEARCHING TRENDS, COLORS, SHAPES, FABRICS

2. DEVELOPING PRODUCT DESIGNS

3. ORDERING SAMPLING FABRICS & TRIMS

4. PATTERNS DEVELOPED

have to perform. The faster and more streamlined your production line is the greater the opportunity for your business to thrive.

While the type of product you have designed will determine the production process, there are key stages that are common to most fashion products.

5. TOILE DEVELOPED

6. PRODUCT SAMPLES CUT & SEWN

7. FINAL SAMPLE COLLECTION SELECTED

8. SELLING SEASON, ORDERS TAKEN & PRODUCTION RUN CALCULATED

9. FINAL PRODUCT MODIFICATIONS MADE

10. PATTERNS GRADED FOR SIZES SOLD

11. PRODUCTION OF ORDER

12. QUALITY-CONTROL CHECKS

13. PACKAGING & SHIPPING

When running any fashion business, the overseeing of the production process is key both to protecting your profit margins and maintaining a high standard of quality across your product

A designer's initial sketch or illustration will be turned into a technical specification drawing before being given to the manufacturer for the final garment to be produced

Research Trends, Colors, Shapes, Fabrics

Chapter 8 explained that trends in fashion can come from many sources: get tuned into as many different ones as possible.

Develop Product Designs

When going into production with manufacturers you will need to supply technical drawings—"specification drawings" or "specs"—to give to the manufacturer on a specification sheet (see above). It is essential that these are accurate and provide enough detail, or the first sample will not be as you intended and can lead to additional costs.

Order Sampling Fabrics and Trims

One of the keys to the success of your product line is your ability to source the correct fabrics and trimmings in the right quantities and at the right price. A full package manufacturer will usually offer assistance in sourcing fabrics. Many designers, however, choose to source their fabrics directly to maintain greater control, while others develop their own fabrics to guarantee uniqueness.

Tips for Shopping at a Fabric Fair

Suzanna Crabb—*Creative Director of designer womenswear label Suzanna*

✖ *Determine the trends you are interested in before visiting, and use the fair as confirmation of existing trends as well as inspiration for new ones.*

✖ *Keep a shopping list of approximately what you are looking for—denim, printed silk, or jersey, for example—as the fairs are vast and allocate certain areas to certain fabrics.*

✖ *Take business cards.*

✖ *Try to visit a fair on the last (or first) day, when it should be quieter, to access stands and have the pick of the cuttings.*

==

Fabric fairs and fabric agents are two common ways to source fabric for your product line. The large international shows, such as Premier Vision and Texworld in Paris, attract large numbers of exhibitors and visitors. Fabric agents work with fabric suppliers on your behalf.

It is advisable as a start-up to order your production fabric only when you know your sales quantities. Many bigger designers will make predictions at the beginning of the season based on previous seasons' sales, but it is a big risk for a small label.

Cut Patterns
The first step in making your samples will be to cut the patterns—these will form the basis of the fit. Poor fit is one of the biggest reasons for fashion product not selling, therefore it is important that either you or the person you outsource to is experienced.

Make Toiles
Toiles are made after the patterns have been cut. Before the first sample is sewn using the correct fabric there is usually a need for a toile—a sample of a garment made in a cheap material so that alterations may be carried out before the garment is produced in the correct material.

Toiles will often have to be adjusted before first samples are produced

Cut and Sew Product Samples

Once the sample fabric has been selected and the first pattern cut it is time to put the product together. Your sample collection is your key tool for both selling and promoting your collection, and must be perfect. If you have overseen the preceding steps carefully there should be no reason for samples to be different from your initial designs, whereas when outsourcing sampling without overseeing it adjustments and modifications will often be necessary.

Select Final Sample Collection

Before you go into your selling period you may need to edit your collection. When your samples come back you may find that individual pieces are not quite working and are reducing the overall impact of the line. It may be best to omit these from your final range.

Take Orders and Calculate the Production Run

At the end of the sales season and when you have confirmed your orders (see Chapter 11) you will need to calculate your production run. This will tell you exactly how many pieces per style and colorway you will need to produce and in what sizes. This will in turn determine the exact quantities of fabric and trims required. A full package manufacturer will have a merchandiser who will take your production run and calculate quantities of fabric and trims. If you are undertaking the production in house, or through a cottage industry or a CMT, it will be your responsibility to calculate everything correctly. You must be careful not to under- or over-order. There are software packages that can help with these calculations.

As well as a spreadsheet of the overall production run, it is also a good idea to hand over a docket or cutting ticket to the manufacturer. This is similar to your earlier specification sheet with all the product details, but includes the quantities of each size going into production.

Make Final Product Modifications

When the sales period has ended you may need to make some final modifications to your product. You must communicate these changes quickly and clearly to your production team. This can mean changing spec drawings or making notes on existing specification sheets. Don't rely on simply telling the team what the changes are. They need to be documented and made available as hard copy.

Grade Patterns for Sizes Sold

Before you began selling your collection you should have decided what sizes you would offer. You need to grade your original patterns up and down to develop patterns for all the sizes you are going into production with.

Produce the Order

You will need to have the role of Production Manager firmly in place to oversee the actual production of the final pieces. In the early days you will probably

When starting out it is common for most designers to have to undertake all of their own quality-control checks as well as packaging and shipping out their orders

undertake this yourself. You will have agreed delivery dates (see Chapter 11) with your buyers and you will be expected to deliver on time and with good quality. This means keeping on top of your production team. Obviously the further away your team is geographically, the harder this can be. Establish a realistic production timeline with your production unit so that you can work out on a weekly and monthly basis if you are on schedule. It is your job to make sure the schedule is adhered to.

Make Quality-Control Checks

Poor quality can be the undoing of new labels. The only failsafe way of guaranteeing quality is to check and double check every single piece.

Your quality-control checks should be happening throughout the production process to identify problems as early as possible. If you find a fault at the end and have to reproduce all the pieces you may jeopardize your delivery date.

Package and Ship

When selling your collection you will have to agree shipping terms with your buyers. It is most common for small labels to place the responsibility for shipping the goods with the stores. This is to protect yourself if anything goes wrong once the goods have left your studio. Make this clear in your terms and conditions when selling. Stores will, however, often issue instructions on how they expect the goods to be delivered. This can include asking for garments to come hanging or flat-packed. Department stores often have very specific guidelines that need to be followed and you will usually have to book in the delivery with them ahead of time. Failure to do this can often result in goods being sent back to you and the cost charged against your order.

If you are selling overseas and have agreed to sell the product at a "landed price," then not only does the responsibility of shipment rest with you but so does the cost of any import duty and tax. Make sure you have costed this into your selling price before agreeing to the terms.

If you are manufacturing your product overseas you will have to arrange delivery of the goods to you. It is worth establishing a relationship with a freight company who will organize the shipment, including paperwork and insurance. It is also worth seeing if you can arrange a credit period with your freight company. This means that they will usually initially cover any import duty and tax and then invoice you for the shipping charge plus tax and duty, giving you a bit of time to pay it off.

Minimums

A minimum is the lowest threshold you can order from a supplier. Minimums exist because the work involved in producing smaller quantities often makes them unprofitable. So, in order to make sure an order leads to a workable profit margin, a supplier puts a minimum order on goods purchased. Minimums most commonly apply to fabric/trim orders and manufacturing quantities.

Minimums can vary hugely, and for fabric orders may range from 20 to 2,000 meters, depending on the supplier, but for the designer sector it will usually start at around 200 meters. For manufacturing you will find CMTs who can offer you anything from one piece per style, usually at a higher price, to full package manufacturers who might start at around 500 pieces per style, but with a significant decrease in cost per unit for larger orders.

Ways Around Minimums

✖ *Offer to pay more:* Although suppliers put minimum orders in place to maximize their profitability you may find that the unit price increase for orders under the minimum may not be that high.

✖ *Ask for stock goods:* Most manufacturers and suppliers will hold on to stock of fabric and finished product, and you may find that minimums are much more relaxed when the stock has already been produced. If you cannot get the exact fabric you require, ask if there is anything similar in stock fabrics. Depending on how unusual your finished product design is, you may find that a supplier has a similar standard product that you can add to.

✖ *Tack your order on:* If you are not able to meet the minimum, ask whether there is a chance of including your order at the end of another major order.

✖ *Creative design:* By cutting down on the styles within your range and offering fewer color options you may meet the minimums required. Otherwise, you could buy a large amount of white fabric and dye it yourself. It is common for designers to make a name for themselves in one fabric for this very reason.

Exclusivity

Suppliers may not be keen to give you exclusivity on a small order. Without exclusivity another major player may come in and get exclusive rights, leaving you hanging out to dry without any product or fabric. You may also find that somebody else is selling exactly the same product as yours at a cheaper price.

Exclusivity tends to become a major issue around recognizable characteristics. Printed fabric is one example and is obviously something that can distinguish your collection from that of a competitor.

Developing your own fabric prints can be a good option, but if you are buying the fabric or product ready-made, ask if anybody else has bought that particular one.

For footwear designer Gil Carvalho, an Italian factory was the natural choice

Sourcing a Manufacturer

 As your sales increase so will the need for you to find a more sizable manufacturing base.

There are many things to consider when outsourcing your production. Fashion start-ups often get themselves into difficulties by not allowing themselves enough time to source their production properly. Take time to consider all of the following:

Location

In an ideal world your manufacturer would be just around the corner from your studio. However, if this is not feasible, start looking as locally as possible. The further you are geographically from your manufacturer the harder communication becomes and the more difficult it is to drop in for a meeting. Sometimes your place of manufacture is dictated by the type of product or even the image you want to project.

As footwear designer Gil Carvalho says, "luxury ladies' shoes are synonymous with Italian production so there was really no choice. We only had to choose the factory most suited to our needs as a company."

If your manufacturer is overseas it's a good idea to take on an agent to supervise the production process. Agents can also help in the sourcing of factories and often work with a number of manufacturers.

Websites such as *www.alibaba.com* offer worldwide sourcing of manufacturers, but you should use them only for initial introductions. You will need to do your research and visit suppliers to make sure they are right for you. You can also contact trade associations in different countries for a list of potential manufacturers.

===

TASKS

1 *Identify three fashion labels whose quality and finish you believe to be excellent. Go to their stockists and look at the garment labels to see where their production is done. Search online or contact the embassy or trade association of that country and ask for a list of manufacturers.*

2 *Look in your local business directory and make a list of seamstresses, tailors, and dry-cleaners. Call around for their rates. Even if you work with a big manufacturer it is always good to have these skills on hand in case of an emergency.*

===

Materials, Machinery, and Production Techniques

You should be working with a manufacturer specializing in the fabrics you are using and with a supplier who can give you access to all you need. Ask for a sample to be made up to demonstrate the standard of workmanship before committing yourself. You may have to pay for this but it will save you a great deal of money and heartbreak in the long run.

If, however, you are bringing fabrics and trims from one country to another, you will need to check the taxes on each of the products being imported. Some countries place very high taxes on the import of certain raw materials to protect their own domestic market.

Quality

The quality of your product is a big factor in the success of your label, and the higher the price point the better the quality should be. In different countries expectations of what constitutes high quality can differ, and this is where samples play an important role. Your sample should be an indicator of the quality you expect when you go into production.

Lead Times

Having agreed delivery dates with your stores you need to be confident that your manufacturer can deliver to you on time. Lead times can vary from factory to factory, with many asking for 60 to 90 days. This will include getting fabrics and trims delivered to them. However, the delivery date will be the date on which the goods are ready to leave them, not the date they will arrive with you. You will then have to factor in time for shipping.

Quantity

Can the manufacturer deliver the quantities you need at the prices you require?

Reliability

You will need your manufacturer to be reliable. When they set a delivery date the goods will need to be ready; when you set a quality standard they must stick to it. You also want to make sure they are a stable business and are going to be around to produce your production run. Ask for references from their other clients.

Negotiation

A manufacturer is not going to make a lot of money out of you until your order quantities really start to rise. As a result you are not the most attractive proposition, and you will find that large numbers of manufacturers will not even entertain working with you. You need to convince manufacturers that you are important and that they should look after your production as well as possible. To do this you can:

✖ Increase your order quantity
✖ Reorder
✖ Pay on time
✖ Let the manufacturer know when you are in the media; they gain kudos by working with a successful company.

Sustainability

As discussed on page 11 a greater number of labels are looking to develop their product using sustainable materials and practices. While this may create more work for you developing and overseeing the production process because of the relative scarcity of fabrics and manufacturers that meet the required ethical standards, it can add value to both your product and brand. Indeed, for many fashion businesses sustainability is at the heart of their brand ethos.

Tips for Start-Up Fashion Labels Wanting to Integrate Sustainable Practices

===

Claire Hamer—founder of Ei8ht

- -

✖ *Do not try to address everything at once. Chose one key "sustainability" hook and ensure you communicate this to the consumer. Any additional elements are a bonus and targets to work toward. You should always explain to the customer that you are on a journey but equally outline the impacts you have had to date.*

✖ *Always make sure you consider the product first, otherwise you will not create desirable collections and therefore will not be sustainable financially. Do not restrict yourself; when you are a new brand it is difficult to find affordable and beautiful sustainable fabrics.*

✖ *Once you have a collection you are proud of, invest in the branding and the way your lookbook is presented. All too often this is neglected.*

✖ *Research what other sustainable brands are doing and how they communicate their message.*

✖ *If you are working with small cooperatives make sure you document what they do with pictures and films and find a stylish way to bring this to your target customer and the media. Everyone loves a story and done in an artistic way this can really grab attention and engage the customer and media.*

✖ *Make sure what you are saying is true—you should reap the rewards of telling an honest, passionate, and engaging story, but don't risk losing everything by not being clear and transparent.*

✖ *If you are struggling to find more sustainable materials but want to introduce a few pieces, consider collaborating with a bigger retailer or brand, as their buying power may open up more options.*

✖ *As materials are particularly challenging, look at the more social side of sustainable sourcing. There are a growing number of fair trade cooperatives that you could work with. These include SOKO in Kenya, who Ei8ht works with for the ASOS Africa collection (www.soko-kenya.com).*

Sustainable fashion by Christopher Raeburn

Terms and Conditions

It is important to agree terms and conditions up front, ideally in the form of a contract, although manufacturers are often reluctant to sign contracts so you may have to rely on verbal agreements or email confirmations. You should look for the following in writing:

Full Manufacturing Agreement
Covers order quantities, shipment, payment, insurance, quality, and delivery dates. It should also prevent the manufacturer selling on your designs to a third party without first discussing it with you and obtaining your agreement.

Agreement for Provision of a Sample
Will you pay for sampling or will it be free if you guarantee to go into production for a certain number of units? Who owns the rights to the sample if you choose not to go into production with the manufacturer?

Confidentiality or Non-Disclosure Agreement
This states that the manufacturer agrees not to discuss your product with anyone or show it to anyone outside of your and the manufacturer's business. As a small label a manufacturer may well work with you for the kudos your name can bring and may want to show off your product to their bigger, more mass-produced clients.

Price and Payment
The manufacturer should usually give you a rough estimate of price based on the specification drawings, then a completed price per style once samples have been made. If you are working with a full package manufacturer this price should be inclusive of everything apart from delivery. You should negotiate this price, as manufacturers will often quote an inflated initial price, expecting you to come in with a lower counter-offer. It is also important to agree the payment terms.

Delivery
Most manufacturers will expect you to look after the shipping of your product from their factory, especially if this involves import or export duty and tax. Make sure you know what your unit price does and doesn't include.

Common Delivery Terms

==

Ex Factory: *The price includes only the cost of the goods and you are responsible for all freight, insurance, duties, and tax incurred in shipping the product. Ownership of the goods transfers to you once the product has been picked up from the factory.*

FOB (Free On Board): *The goods will be deemed to be delivered to you at the point that the goods pass the ship's rail. Obviously, this will normally be as the goods are swung on to the ship in their container.*

CIF (Cost, Insurance, and Freight): *The manufacturer is providing a price inclusive of the cost of goods, the insurance for their journey to their destination port/unloading point, and the cost of whichever method of freight is being used to transport the goods to you.*

CFR or C&F (Cost and Freight): *The manufacturer is providing a price which includes the cost of the goods and of the freight, but not insurance.*

LDP (Landed Duty Paid): *The price includes goods, insurance, freight, and the duties and quotas associated with importing the product.*

==

Manufacturing will be an ongoing process for your fashion label and is therefore something you need to get your head around quickly. It can be the most time-consuming aspect of running your business, especially if you are creating a new and exciting collection two, three, or even four times a year. You will find that at the same time as making sure samples are arriving on time and to specification, the production of the previous season's orders will need overseeing and sending out.

Give yourself 12 to 18 months to sort out your entire supply chain so that you are confident when you take your product to market for the first time that you have an infrastructure in place that will allow you to maximize the potential of your business. Don't be in a rush and never assume that your production will take care of itself.

Production Calendar (Northern Hemisphere)

Month	Spring/Summer 2013	Fall/Winter 2013
March 2012	Research fabric Start designs	
April 2012	Select fabrics Order fabrics	
May 2012	Create patterns Begin sampling	
June 2012	Collections developed	
July 2012	Establish production plan Finish sampling	
August 2012	Sales season begins	
September 2012	Collections shown Sales continue	Research fabric Start designs
October 2012	Order books close	Select fabrics Order fabrics
November 2012	Production materials ordered Production starts	Create patterns Begin sampling
December 2012	Oversee production	Collections developed
January 2013	Oversee production	Establish production plan Finish sampling
February 2013	Product arrives Deliver to stores	Sales season begins
March 2013	Continuation of deliveries Chasing of monies owed	Collections shown Sales continue
April 2013		Order books close
May 2013		Production materials ordered Production starts
June 2013		Oversee production
July 2013		Oversee production
August 2013		Product arrives Deliver to stores
September 2013		Continuation of deliveries Chasing of monies owed

Case Study: Christopher Raeburn

Christopher Raeburn is a young British fashion designer who has become known for his pioneering concept of creating ethically aware, innovative mens- and womenswear collections from re-appropriated military fabrics. After graduating with an MA from the Royal College of Art in 2006, he freelanced as a pattern cutter before launching his eponymous label two years later.

Everything Christopher designs is made from redeployed military fabrics so it is all recycled. However, he is quick to point out that the product has "a very different aesthetic to most ethical designers." He started working with these fabrics while an undergraduate and experimented with different upcycled garments, honing his techniques. "I have always had a fascination for military fabrics and their functional qualities." His reasons are twofold: firstly "it is functional and waterproof" and secondly, "the inherent thing with the military is that they have to overproduce to ensure that there is enough kit for every eventuality." This means that there "is an incredible amount of stock barely used." By tapping into this resource Christopher has used an array of materials: "we have worked with parachutes, wool battledress jackets, fire trousers, ponchos, tents… the list goes on."

All of Christopher's designs are made in the UK in his small east London production facility. He uses the terminology "Remade in England" to promote the concept behind the label. " 'Remade in England' helps to explain the backbone of my business in the UK. We will completely deconstruct the old garments and then 'remake' them into new, contemporary outerwear garments. I spend a lot of time researching the supply." He has used military fabrics from the UK, Germany, the Czech Republic, as well as from former East Germany, "which has a post-cold war feeling." His biggest challenge "is to find quantities to make my production scalable, to be able to make 100–200 garments, not a handful."

Christopher is quick to point out that he didn't intend to start out as a sustainable designer but in fact "it's a very happy accident." The primary focus has always been "good design, produced in England." The ethical part "came out of my creative work, and of wanting to use this particular fabric." However, Christopher is now considered one of the leading new breed of ethical fashion designers and

was the first winner of the Ethical Fashion Forum Innovation Award, which set out to find and promote emerging design talent. Entries are judged on the basis of outstanding design and product quality, as well as social and environmental innovation. As part of the award Christopher was offered a free space to exhibit through an installation at Estethica, London Fashion Week's platform for sustainability, which served as the showcase for the launch of his label. Christopher has used installations as a way of helping to promote his work, and he has also been asked by Liberty, London and Barneys, New York to create visually stunning presentations of his work.

Along the way Christopher has accessed support to develop his business. He won the highly regarded British Fashion Council NEWGEN sponsorship, offering him free space to present his men's and women's collections at the main London Fashion Week exhibition twice a year and also take part in the London Showrooms selling event held in Paris and New York twice a year. He has also received mentoring from former Selfridges and Harrods Creative Director Susanne Tide-Frater as part of the British Fashion Council's Eco Mentoring Scheme. Christopher was successful in applying for the Center For Fashion Enterprise's (CFE) Venture Program, London's pioneering business development platform for emerging fashion designers. The CFE provided bespoke business support with an experienced business development team as well as free studio space. Christopher says "the CFE has been instrumental in the acceleration of my business on a day-to-day level. The strategic and managerial support has helped to ensure that my business is now well organized."

For Christopher, integrity in the design process is everything. Winner of the prestigious British Fashion Awards Emerging Designer of the Year for Menswear 2011, he gains great satisfaction from "giving a piece of clothing a completely new life" and the fact that worldwide "customers have really understood the work that I do; I'm incredibly proud."

Through innovative design and use of re-appropriated fabrics Christopher Raeburn has become a leading figure in the world of sustainable fashion

*S*elling is about talking to people and building trusting, long-lasting relationships. People buy from people they like—depending on your selling strategy you may get only two chances a year in which to meet with buyers, so it is important to get it right first time. You must also be able to talk about your own product convincingly. This chapter looks at all aspects of fashion wholesaling and retailing, at the potential for licensing agreements, and at all the administrative details that are part and parcel of the selling process.

The Sales Window

Before you work out when exactly you will be undertaking the sales of your collection you must have decided on your sales strategy. Will you be wholesaling, retailing, or both?

The Wholesale Sales Window

For most fashion wholesalers the selling period will be dictated by the spring/summer and fall/winter collections, with two sales windows a year lasting between two and four months each. This is when the store buyers will have their budget for the new collections. If you can replenish your goods throughout the season, allowing stores to reorder, additional selling periods will be available to you. The dates for the menswear and womenswear collections are slightly different, with the men's collections usually being shown first.

Pre-collections are presented up to three months ahead of the main seasonal catwalk presentations and are becoming increasingly important to the economic survival of the sector. They are often slightly more wearable and affordable than the catwalk collections—a response by the designer market to the success achieved by the fast fashion model of the retail chains. Many high-end buyers do not want to wait for the seasonal catwalk shows to take place before placing orders, as deliveries of these collections often arrive too late in the season for their core customers. As the high-end shopper is usually keen to have the clothes before anyone else, buyers know that they need to get the collections in store just before the shopping season begins in earnest. Pre-collections allow the store to sell great designer collections earlier, while giving the designer the creative freedom to keep the catwalk collection as inspirational as possible.

Buying appointment at the Magic trade fair, Las Vegas

Wholesale Sales Calendar (Northern Hemisphere)

Pre-collection fall/winter	December
Main collection fall/winter	January through April
Pre-collection spring/summer	July
Main collection spring/summer	August through November

Depending on your product you may also find that a market exists for year-round sales, and your stockists want the opportunity to come back to you from time to time to replenish their stock. This means that you may have to hold some stock or else have a very tight supply chain with short lead times.

The Retail Sales Window

The retail sales window is also driven by seasons, and stock should arrive in stores three to six months later than the wholesale window. For the designer sector it is usual for the spring/summer collections to arrive in stores around January/February, while the fall/winter collections hit the rails in August/September. The more mass market your product the greater the opportunity for shorter but more frequent sales seasons, when the product hits the shop floor at exactly the time of year it is intended to be worn (see the fast fashion model on page 17).

Wholesaling

Fashion wholesalers sell goods to a third party who will sell the goods on to the consumer. If you will need a boutique or department store or an online marketplace such as *www.net-a-porter.com* to sell your goods to the consumer, even if it is only a few pieces, you will be considered a wholesaler.

The biggest advantage of wholesaling is that you can limit your initial stock investment to the order quantities placed by stores. So, before you purchase your goods from your manufacturer you already know exactly how many pieces you will require, in which styles, colors, and sizes.

The biggest disadvantage is that you are not getting the full retail value of your goods (see Chapter 13).

There are three main reasons why many fashion start-ups choose the wholesale route:

Limited funds: Fashion retailing can mean greater overheads, including investment in stock. Many new fashion labels simply cannot afford to retail.

Distribution: Wholesaling gives you the potential to be represented in hundreds of stores worldwide, making your label instantly accessible to many potential customers.

Your collection needs to be well presented at all times to maximize the chances of buyers picking up your label for their stores

Credibility: An established retailer who chooses your label to be represented in their shop is telling customers that you are worthy of their attention.

Studio Sales

As a new fashion business, getting buyers to come to you can be tricky. Your lookbooks and other marketing materials (see Chapter 12) are there to entice the buyer into making an appointment with you. They serve as an introduction to your label and the new collection. However, buyers see hundreds of lookbooks each season, so you will need to build relationships with them by cold calling to introduce yourself, make sure they received your lookbook and marketing materials, and ask for an appointment.

Make sure your studio sends out the right message and is presented well, and that the collection looks fantastic. Be tidy and be prepared—fresh flowers always look good. Offer the buyers a drink and make sure you have enough seating. Making them welcome and comfortable is an important part of building a good and lasting relationship.

Rejection is part and parcel of the selling game. Established stores may not be looking for any new collections. Even if they are looking to drop one or two lines they have hundreds of collections from which to choose. You may be lucky and have the right product at the right time, but for most new fashion labels it's a case of slowly building your reputation with these stores until the time is right for them to buy. Don't take a "no" personally, and remember that it doesn't mean "no" forever. After a few seasons, when the buyer has seen your product and press for a while, they may be ready to stock you. Be persistent.

Exhibitions

Exhibitions give buyers a good opportunity to see many different collections under one roof in a short period of time. Choosing the right exhibition is key— you can't afford to spend money on the wrong one. Do your research. Which exhibitions do your competitors attend? Ask the organizers for their exhibitor and buyer attendance lists from previous seasons. Talk with other fashion businesses that have attended in previous seasons. You don't want to sign up for an exhibition based solely on the previous exhibitor lists only to find that poor buyer attendance means those exhibitors are no longer showing.

Exhibitions play a massive role in the sales strategy of most wholesale fashion labels. Research exhibitions thoroughly and work out which one is best for your label before committing yourself

The exhibition organizers decide which fashion labels participate and they will work hard to protect the reputation of their event. You must present yourself professionally. Any pre-launch press you have achieved will be impressive. If you already have stockists you will be bringing buyers to the exhibition. It may take a few seasons to be accepted, especially into one of the bigger exhibitions with established brands. However, once you have been accepted you will need to think about how you will present your collection.

You must keep to a tight budget in the first season. This means not taking on too big a stand. However, you will need a stand that is large enough to show off your collection in a professional and visually stimulating manner. Make sure you have enough rail space—but not too much. Most exhibitions have minimum stand sizes. Accessories labels can often take a smaller stand than clothing labels, as their product often takes up less space, especially if it is jewelry. Check with the organizers.

You must present your collection professionally—make sure your hangers are all the same and attach swing tickets to each item.

Try to create an enticing space that leaves the buyer some room for interpretation. You want them to come on to your stand with an open mind. There will probably be something there for them whether their store has a minimalist or French boudoir theme.

Send out lookbooks with details of where you will be exhibiting and which stand you will be on. Many buyers go to exhibitions to meet with their existing customers rather than to look for new labels. If they do have a look around the exhibition they should already have been introduced to your label. This increases the likelihood of name and product recognition and may persuade them to have a look though your collection.

Buyers from big stores often travel in packs. They will know exactly what they are looking for and will attend specific shows, like Magic in Las Vegas, where they are guaranteed to see a number of interesting brands relevant to their market

Position tables and chairs to maximize the potential of your space. The stand needs to be functional but exciting. A changing room can be very helpful for buyers who want to see how things fit. If you can, stretch your budget to a fit model (a model who is the perfect size for your product samples).

Types of Buyers

Buyers range from those who know what they want (department stores and established boutiques) to those just starting, who can be a little overwhelmed. Others will be keen to buy but need your guidance. Some buyers will love your collection while others will not be at all interested. You will also find some time-wasters who will go through the collection at length but never place an order. Don't allow anyone to take pictures of your collection before they place an order unless they are from a reputable store or have a press pass (after a few seasons you will recognize who's who). It is common for buyers to want to see you for a few seasons before placing their first order. They will want to see continuity and growth before making the decision to bring you on board.

Buyers will often give feedback, whether they are buying or not. It is worth listening to it, even if it's a little harsh. You will quickly find that different buyers will like and dislike different things, quite often contradicting each other on what needs to be changed. Write everything down. However, do not feel you have to throw everything out of the window and start again from scratch. Buyers will most often be talking about what is right for their specific customers and it may be that you have not met the right buyers yet. Being true to yourself and your creativity is an important part of establishing your label's identity.

Always get business cards from buyers and make a note on the back of when and where you met, together with any feedback.

Exhibiting Overseas

It is often recommended not to exhibit overseas until you have some revenue coming in to cover the additional costs. However, some young fashion businesses who do not do well in their domestic market do fantastically well in the overseas markets. Taking part in exhibitions abroad will often add credibility—telling a buyer that you exhibit in London, Paris, Milan, and New York suggests that you must already have achieved some success.

Talk to other designers about their experience and to the government department responsible for exporting and doing business in different countries. You may even be eligible for a grant.

The Art of Selling

===

Step 1: Set objectives
You need clearly defined objectives that are measurable over a specific timeframe. When setting your objectives initially, consider your "break-even" point and what revenue is needed to continue functioning. Break this down into a seasonal sales target. Later you can aim to increase last season's sales turnover by a specific amount.

Step 2: Prospecting
Prospecting is the process of looking for new leads to sell to. Continual research of new boutiques and stores is needed to maximize the number of potential customers. Allocate time to finding new customers as well as building up a database of loyal buyers.

Step 3: Qualifying
This is the art of sorting the qualified prospects from the unqualified. Out of your 20 new leads, which ones are truly ready now to buy your type of product at the price you are asking? This process will save you a great deal of time, enabling you to focus on building relationships with strong prospects rather than chasing those that are not willing or able to buy.

Step 4: The sales process
The sales process is all about building a relationship of trust and a rapport between you and your buyers. People like doing business with people they like, especially in small businesses. Get them excited about some key pieces in the collection and build from there. When talking through your product, remember to sell the benefits in a way your buyer can appreciate and that is tailored to their specific business interests, whether it be in terms of style or the bottom line.

Step 5: Follow up
After the sale has been closed and the buyer has placed an order, following up the sale is imperative to building a long-term relationship. A note to say it was great meeting them, periodic calls to let them know how delivery is going, clippings of any press that has been achieved, will help to make buyers feel they have made the right choice. Once the goods have been delivered, it's always good to follow up to see if everything is OK and check how the collection is selling.

===

Sales Agents

If you feel that you are not the person to take on the selling of your collection you could hand it over to an agent. An agent may take one or more collections to the buyers. Agents might also have a space to show the collection or even take a stand at exhibitions. They should have a list of already established clients, so you may be able to piggyback on someone else's relationship.

An agent does not purchase the product from you but merely meets new and existing stockists on your behalf. Most work on a commission basis, usually from zero to 15 percent of all sales depending on the product (traditionally for footwear collections this is 5–8 percent, handbags 3–5 percent, apparel 8–15 percent). The general rule is that if the agent brings a buyer to you that is ready, willing, and able to purchase the products at the stated price, the agent will be entitled to receive a commission regardless of whether the relationship between you and the buyer is consummated. However, to decrease the risk that a commission must be paid for orders that don't come to fruition, the agent's commission may be calculated and paid, in decreasing risk to you, only upon:

✖ Orders accepted by you
✖ Orders produced by you
✖ Orders shipped by you
✖ Orders delivered to the buyer by you
✖ Deliveries accepted by the buyer
✖ Deliveries paid by the buyer
✖ Proceeds of sales collected by you.

You are responsible for distribution, and an agent will pass all the orders, contracts, and shipping details to you.

Before taking you on, an agent has to feel confident that you will sell enough to make the relationship worthwhile. Quite often they will want to see that you have been trading for a few seasons and have picked up some stockists from which they can grow your business.

It is advisable that a contract appointing a sales agent should contain the following, in addition to a description of the products involved: agreed territory; time frame; termination clauses—these need to be established at the beginning of the relationship when you and your representative are on good terms; review clauses—set dates for reviewing the agreement and state what will be reviewed; and performance targets; but you should always consult an attorney before entering into such an agreement:

✖ The agent should not have the right to assume liabilities on your behalf
✖ The agent cannot accept orders from buyers; instead they must be submitted to you and you then decide whether to accept them or not
✖ The agent does not have control of the products and, therefore, bears no risk if the products are lost
✖ Any breach of contract between you and the buyer does not affect the right of the agent to receive their commission
✖ The list of customers created by the agent on your behalf becomes your property

✖ At the termination of the agreement the agent is not entitled to any payment for goodwill or increased business generated by the agent, other than any commission due

✖ You should cautiously describe the limitations of the agent's authority, so that they may not negotiate prices, delivery schedules, terms and conditions of sales, discounts, warranties, and return policies

✖ You should also describe any additional duties of the agent (beyond using their best efforts to promote your collection) including attending trade shows or providing assurances of credit worthiness of customers, for example.

Distributors

Using a distributor is quite common when selling in overseas markets where language can be problematic. The distributor is your sole client for the agreed region and places one big order with you, taking responsibility for liaising with the stores, including over delivery and payment. The distributor purchases the product from you and then sells it on, most often marking up your supply price (although some may negotiate a percentage of sales, ranging from 2 to 12 percent, depending on your potential sales turnover), to cover additional in-market costs of ownership distribution and invoicing/debt-recovery. The distributor will take on all after-sales service and will help pay for and undertake promotion of your collection in the agreed market.

A distribution agreement may contain the following specific conditions. Again, you should consult an attorney before entering into such an agreement:

✖ The distributor may want assurances and the assumption of liability from you in the event that you lose ownership of your brand or trademark. This is because such an event would bring all their efforts to nothing

✖ Usually the distributor owns the customer's list of clients in the agreed geographic area

✖ On the other hand, you might seek to ensure that the distributor reveals the names of customers for each order to you

✖ You may segregate some customers in the territory from the agreement and continue to supply them yourself. In this case, you may need to pay the distributor a commission on such sales to compensate them for loss of business

✖ You may allow the distributor to maintain a warehouse of stock, overstocking on some lines that they consider will do particularly well to allow them to fulfill repeat orders.

Agency v Distributorship

==

Advantages of an agent:

✖ *Agents can have very good market expertise and their own ready-made client base*

✖ *An agent usually charges an agreed commission (around 10 percent on all sales), so selling costs are known in advance and can be built into pricing*

✖ *You usually pay an agent after the buyer has paid you*

✖ *You retain control over your branding as you are responsible for marketing and promotion.*

Disadvantages of an agent:

✖ *You are responsible for all deliveries of goods, which, if selling in many countries, can result in a relatively complex distribution process*

✖ *The agent is unlikely to be involved in funding promotional activity and does not usually undertake marketing or promotion of your product. Some agencies offer press and marketing services separately for a monthly retainer*

✖ *The credit risk falls to you; however, because you usually pay the agent after you have been paid, the agent may well follow up payment on your behalf.*

Advantages of a distributor:

✖ *You've got only one customer (the distributor)*

✖ *The distributor is responsible for the credit risk of all sales*

✖ *The distributor holds your stock in-market (i.e., in the sales territory for which they are responsible)*

✖ *The distributor helps pay for and undertakes marketing and promotion of your product in the market*

✖ *The distributor develops a customer base for your product.*

Disadvantages of a distributor:

✖ *The distributor has complete control of the selling process; you have none*

✖ *The cost of selling through a distributor may force the product out of market competition—a distributor may add up to 50 percent mark-up (or even more) to your product before it reaches the retailer*

✖ *You may not know who your customers are*

✖ *Because a distributor shares responsibility for marketing and promotion, you may not retain total control over the branding of your product*

✖ *Distributors who are wholesalers (rather than specialized master distributors) may not sell effectively to other wholesalers*

✖ *Your distributor may not have the sales force for new product introductions in larger markets*

✖ *Your distributor's time and attention may be spread over multiple products.*

===

Licensing Agreements

In a license you, as the owner of the brand (the licensor), give another party (the licensee) permission to design, manufacture, and market products using your brand, in exchange for a royalty. By doing so you will be able to expand your brand into other product categories in which you may have no manufacturing or sales expertise, and the licensee is able to add value to their product while gaining access to your loyal customer base. Many designer labels lend their names to a variety of products, with perfumes being the major money-spinner for fashion brands. Donna Karan, Ralph Lauren, Chanel, Alexander McQueen, and Paul Smith all have a number of licensing agreements for the production and distribution of selected products.

Before entering into a licensing agreement you will need to consider, however, how much of your input is required and how much control you will retain. It can all depend on the agreement. The most serious caveat in a licensing agreement is undoubtedly the potential loss of control over quality, design, and marketing strategy.

You will need to show any contracts to your attorney to make sure you are getting a good deal as well as doing enough to protect your brand.

Exclusivity

Stores may ask for a certain amount of exclusivity with your collection, ranging from total exclusivity (you sell only in their store), to regional exclusivity (you agree not to sell within a certain geographical area around their store). It is up to you to determine how important the store is for you. If they have more than 100 outlets and you will be doing a lot of business with them, total exclusivity for a specific period of time may be an option. If you are a designer label you may want to maintain the exclusiveness of your product. Selling to too many stores in a small town may make your label too accessible and devalue the brand. On the other hand, you don't want to agree to anything that is not going to allow your business to develop a healthy client base and turnover. Think very carefully before agreeing any exclusivity.

The Paperwork

You will need to get all your paperwork ready for the selling season.

Order forms

When a buyer is ready to place an order you will need an order form that captures all of the information necessary to process the order. It must include:
* Your label's details, including who has taken the order
* The customer's details, including any tax numbers and billing address
* Date
* Order number
* A description of each style
* Quantity of each style, colorways, sizes, and price
* Delivery address
* Delivery date.

The delivery date is the date the goods will leave you, not the date they will arrive with the customer. While you can be confident about when the goods will be packed and ready for shipping at your studio, you don't know how long a courier or shipper is going to take (you don't want to be responsible for any unforeseen shipping delays). Unless you have agreed a "landed" selling price (whereby the cost of each unit sold includes delivery to the customer's door), the delivery and shipping costs and arrangements will be carried by the customer (see page 126 for a list of shipping terminology). It is quite common for designers to give the stores a delivery window during which the goods will arrive. This allows you to prioritize certain styles in your production run that you feel should be in the stores first or that your key stockists have ordered.

Paul Smith has grown his eponymous label by working with Japanese licensing partner Itochu

Typical Delivery Dates for Seasonal Collections (Northern Hemisphere)

Menswear fall/winter	August
Womenswear fall/winter	August and September
Menswear spring/summer	January
Womenswear spring/summer	Late January through February

You will also need to let buyers know when you will be closing your order books for the season—they may want to make some changes or think about numbers before signing.

Either have duplicate forms made up or print off two copies and keep one copy, giving the other to the buyer for reference.

Terms and conditions

It is imperative that you include the terms and conditions of sale on the back of your order form. This lets the buyers know exactly what they are agreeing to when signing the form. Have your attorney look over any terms and conditions you set out to make sure you are covering yourself fully.

New customer form

It is good practice to ask new customers to fill out a new customer form, especially if they are looking for credit.

Confirmation

This is the final contract between you and the store before you go into production. This is also the time that you can invoice for your deposit if this has been agreed to. Never go into production before the confirmation is signed.

Once you have closed your order books you need to work out your production run for the season. This means looking to see if there are any styles or colorways that you have not sold enough of to go into production. Before you send out confirmation to a buyer whose order you are canceling for this reason, call and explain. You want to be able to produce everything that was ordered, but this is not always possible—especially in the early days when sales volume may be low.

Payment terms

It is up to you to establish payment terms with each of your customers. There are several options open to you (terminology can differ depending on the country you are selling to).

✖ **Deposit:** Ideally you would like to receive a deposit on the order when the confirmation has been signed. Anything from 25 to 50 percent would be the norm. This should cover the costs of the goods produced if the store reneges on its order. It is more common to receive deposits from new customers for the first couple of seasons, and it is almost impossible to get deposits from the big department stores.

✖ **Pre-payment:** You can ask for the balance to be paid before the goods are sent for delivery. This will help with your cash flow. It is also a good way of getting stores to pay promptly, as any delay in payment means they have empty rails and lose valuable selling time.

- ✖ **COD (Cash on Delivery):** This is the reverse of the pre-payment option. You send the goods to the customer who pays on receipt. If you are unfamiliar with a store ask for a money order or a direct bank transfer. (Ask your bank which payment methods will cost you less. Online banking is often cheaper.)

- ✖ **NET Terms:** This is where you give a period of credit before payment is due. NET 30, which is a very standard payment term, gives the customer 30 days from the date of the invoice to pay. You can ask for a deposit upfront and then the remainder of the balance NET 30. Payment terms can vary from country to country—Italy will commonly ask for NET 60 or NET 90, which can mean waiting two to three months for payment. For most new fashion start-ups terms like these will be very difficult, as cash flow is so important to the survival of the business. Larger department stores will often dictate their payment terms, often taking a 3 to 5 percent discount if they pay within the agreed time period. You will have to decide whether or not you can live with the loss of revenue and how important the store is to you in terms of profile-raising and turnover.

COMPANY LOGO

Order Form
Company Contact Details

Order No:

Order Taken By:

Sales Tax No:

Contact Name:	
Co. Name:	
Date:	
Address:	
Tel:	
Fax:	
Cell:	
Email Address:	
Payment Terms:	
Shipping Details:	
Delivery Address:	
Delivery Date:	

Style No.	Description	Color/Print	XS 4	S 6	M 8	L 10	Qty	Unit Cost ($)	Total Cost ($)

Comments:		NET TOTAL	
		SALES TAX	
		TOTAL	

The supply of the garments stated here is made subject to the conditions set out on the reverse hereof, acknowledgment of which is evidenced by the signature of the Purchaser.

Signature:

Date:

✖ ***Consignment/Sale or Return:*** These two payment terms are often confused by small designers and boutiques alike. While both arrangements afford the buyer the right to return goods to the supplier if not sold, "sale or return" constitutes an actual sale, with ownership of the goods being transferred to the stockist. With a consignment deal the goods remain the property of the supplier at all times and the buyer has an option to take title to the goods in the event the goods are sold on to a third party. Both options, although attractive to retailers, can prove to be a massive burden for many young labels' cashflow and should be considered very carefully.

✖ ***Letter of credit:*** The store establishes credit with a local bank, clearly describing the goods to be purchased, the price, the documentation required, and a time limit for completion of the transaction. On receipt of the letter of credit you release the goods to the store. Most stores are reluctant to pay by this method, as it is expensive to set up.

✖ ***Credit card:*** For smaller stores this can sometimes be a welcome alternative, if you have the facility. You will need to factor in the charge the credit card companies will deduct from all payments made, typically anywhere between 1 and 5 percent.

COMPANY LOGO									**Invoice**	

COMPANY NAME

COMPANY ADDRESS

Invoice No:

Date:

CUSTOMER

Customer's Name

Customer's Address

STYLE NO	NAME	MAIN FABRIC	XS	S	M	L	Qty	Unit Price $	Total Price $

	Sub Total	
	Sales Tax	
	Delivery	
	TOTAL	

PAYMENT TERMS

BANK DETAILS FOR PAYMENT

COMPANY NO:	SALES TAX NO:

Harrods, one of the world's most renowned retailers, is an example of a classic department store

Smaller labels often have a number of different payment options with their customers, many of whom are small retailers. The more you work with a store the more you will trust them and the better the terms you might then offer them.

To receive payment you will need to invoice your customers. Invoices (see opposite) must include the date and your:

- ✖ Business name
- ✖ Trading name
- ✖ Logo

- ✖ Address and contact details
- ✖ Tax numbers (including Sales Tax)
- ✖ Invoice number

Invoices must also include your customer's:

- ✖ Company name
- ✖ Trading name
- ✖ Address and contact details
- ✖ Tax numbers (including Sales Tax)
- ✖ Item reference
- ✖ Item detail

- ✖ Price/item
- ✖ Total price
- ✖ Applicable tax per item
- ✖ Total price per item
- ✖ Total price, total tax
- ✖ Amount payable.

They should also detail the date of the invoice, your payment methods, including your bank account number, or "check payable to," payment terms, and status of payment. Check with your accountant to make sure you have everything required by law.

Retailing

The biggest advantage of retailing your own product is the obvious opportunity to make bigger profit margins. There are other advantages, depending on what type of retail method you choose.

Your Own Store

Having your own shop is something all designers aspire to, and it can help with the wholesale side of your business as well. It offers buyers an opportunity to see your complete brand concept under one roof and also gives them confidence that you have a sellable product. The high risk and cost involved, however, usually means that fashion start-ups stay away from this option until they are established.

Although most fashion retailers start up as one-off boutiques, the different types of retailers include department stores, specialty stores, boutiques, chain stores, and discount stores.

The type of retailer you will aim to be will be determined by your retail theory. This will depend on your product, your ideal customer, and the potential size of your store. Your options are:

1 **Low mark-up with high volume and huge selection** (retail chain mass market retailer)
2 **Higher mark-up with lower volume but with full selection** (department store)
3 **High mark-up with low volume and smaller selection** (boutique).

Now think about location (see pages 84–5).

E-commerce

The past 10 to 15 years have seen a massive revolution in the way that we shop. Selling directly via the internet was once seen within fashion circles as a no-no. The belief that consumers would want to touch and feel fabrics and try products on before purchase was always cited as a reason why online shopping for fashion and clothing in particular would never take off. However, the success of online fashion retailers like *asos.com*, *figleaves.com*, and *net-a-porter.com* has proved the doubters wrong.

Online shopping continues to see an increase year on year with consumers happier than ever to buy direct from a multi brand or own brand website. In 2010, UK shoppers spent more than £50bn online, and this figure will only rise. While leaders in the field like *asos.com* and *net-a-porter.com* have already been trading online for ten years, two of the biggest retailers, Zara and Gap, only launched their e-commerce sites in 2010, showing that even the big boys can be late in adopting what is one of the most potentially profitable routes to market for any fashion label.

A well-presented and functionally sound e-commerce platform (like *goodsie.com*) offers start-ups a great opportunity for direct retail to consumers at a relatively affordable price. Bricks and mortar stores are too costly for many start-ups and they can be restrictive for niche brands due to their fixed geographical location. A finite number of consumers will want to buy your label, and they may be dotted around the world rather than within reach of your store. Online selling offers young labels the opportunity to engage with a global client base and develop a loyal following no matter where the consumer lives. It is also worth bearing in mind that according to a PayPal online report e-retail is expected to grow by more than 36 percent by 2012, compared to just 1 percent for in-store sales until the end of 2012.

More and more fashion start-ups see e-commerce as their primary means of selling from the outset. The internet also provides a readily available marketing facility, in the form of social media sites such as Facebook and Twitter, which can be used to promote own brand sites and engage with shoppers worldwide.

The Essentials

James Vanderzee, owner of Vie Digital, an e-commerce and digital marketing agency, explains that there are a number of obvious opportunities for small fashion businesses online. "Most fashion businesses' customers are already online, there is a lower cost of sale and therefore bigger margins, and it's a 24/7 opportunity; you have the potential to make money while you sleep."

The Online Fashion Brand's Bare Essentials (see diagram on page 147)

==

James Vanderzee—*CEO of Vie Digital* (www.viedigital.com/fashion)

Getting online
Testing your proposition online.

- ✖ **Web address:** *Buy a relevant and memorable domain.*
- ✖ **Hosting:** *Arrange server space for your website to live.*
- ✖ **Holding page:** *While your site is being built set up a holding page with contact details.*
- ✖ **Product showcase:** *Add a "brochure" or gallery element to your website.*
- ✖ **"Share" tools:** *Add some social media plug-ins such as AddThis.com.*
- ✖ **Web tracking:** *Get some website tracking in place so you can monitor how many visitors are coming to your site, and where they are coming from.*
- ✖ **Content management:** *Make sure your website allows you to manage the content (text, imagery, etc.) yourself via an easy-to-use Content Management System (CMS).*

The Customer Journey

The Customer Journey and Related E-commerce Process

The customer journey
The chart above shows the stages of a customer's journey from visiting the site to buying (in pink), and how each stage should relate to your e-commerce process (shown in blue).

Selling online

Earning money while you sleep. Every good e-commerce process includes:

✖ *A product brochure*
✖ *A shopping basket*
✖ *Customer accounts (sign up/log in)*
✖ *Payment processing*
✖ *Delivery and fulfillment*
✖ *Returns management*
✖ *Up-to-date stock control*
✖ *Excellent customer service throughout.*

Remember:

✖ *E-commerce is multi-platform: your customers will want to buy via their smart phones as well as via their computers so your website must be able to support these.*
✖ *You need to plan for fulfillment of overseas sales: selling online is a global opportunity so you need options for delivery to the other side of the world, as well as locally.*
✖ *Account for returns in your budgeting (and Terms & Conditions): with regional sizing variations, returns could potentially be as much as half of all your sales.*
✖ *Weigh up your payment options carefully: you can be charged in a number of different ways, from monthly fees to percentages of the transaction value. If you're starting off, speak to your bank about an e-merchant account or go for a solution like PayPal or Google Checkout.*
✖ *Ensure you have efficient e-commerce processes in place: check all systems and ensure that everyone involved in your sales process knows what to do once the order has been received, is ready for delivery, and needs returning.*

Promoting online

If you build it will they come? Be where your customers (and competitors) are:

✖ *Web directories and related third party websites. Find any websites that your customers and competitors are using and, where possible, ensure you also have a presence there.*
✖ *Use Paid Search advertising:*
   – *Google AdWords ("buy" keywords relating to your brand and products to ensure that you appear on page 1 of Google for those search terms)*
   – *Facebook Ads (promote your brand and products to people who are fans of similar brands on Facebook)*
✖ *Search Engine Optimization (SEO): create plenty of keyword-optimized content on your website and on other websites about your brand and products, and generate as many relevant links to your website as possible, to help boost your performance on the search engines as well as generate real human traffic to your site.*
✖ *Social media, blogging, and online PR are a big part of SEO. These activities will generate content and links, and they also have great potential in helping to promote awareness of your brand and interest in your products and in generating real human traffic and sales.*

Retaining online
How do you retain existing business?

- ✖ *Add more product, news, and blog content*
- ✖ *Invite participation*
- ✖ *Engage via a Facebook business page*
- ✖ *Communicate to followers on Twitter*
- ✖ *Email newsletters to customers on database*
- ✖ *Promote online and offline activities.*

==

Markets

Choosing the right market says a lot about your business. The higher in price you go the more this becomes a concern. You need to make sure the market you are selling from has a reputation for supporting designer labels.

Private Clients

Many labels start off making one-off pieces or a small sample range that they are then able to offer clients in their exact measurements. The bonus of this is that you can ask for payments to be made in stages, the first of which (deposit) should be enough to cover the cost of making. This means your initial outlay is covered. Private clients can come to you, or you can go to them. This service works well for people who are cash-rich but time-poor.

Yoga-inspired fashion label KokoFlow used the Yoga Show (a consumer trade show) to launch the label and gain invaluable feedback from prospective customers

Consumer Shows

Consumer events usually take place over a short period and you will be charged for taking up a stall at the event. Ally Ward from yoga clothing collection KokoFlow says, "Before the show I had called around everyone who exhibited there the year before so I knew what to expect, and the most useful advice was not to go overboard on spending. I kept costs low and made a simple, bright, eye-catching stand. I went with the idea in mind that what I wanted most was feedback. I found it invaluable talking to customers, buyers, and even other sellers. I got loads of information, contacts, and had a total blast. As a bonus I made some sales, but not being hung up on that at my first show made everything so much better."

Television

Home shopping networks such as QVC and the Home Shopping Channel offer a huge client base for the right fashion labels and can deliver a great deal of business if the product is right.

House Parties

Home shopping parties have moved on a long way since the early Tupperware parties and can prove a viable option for selling your product directly to your customer. Even major fashion retailers like Topshop are getting in on the act with their "Topshop to Go" service, which they advertise as "a mobile style service aiming to provide the ultimate in home shopping."

Trunk Shows

This could involve taking a room in a hotel in a major city where you know your collection will be well received, going to corporate businesses who want to offer their employees something unique during their lunch break, or setting up at a country club to offer members a special chance to meet the designer and buy the product direct. Some department stores also offer the opportunity for up-and-coming labels to hold trunk shows in their stores.

Sample Sales

Taking part in sample sales throughout the year (if you have the stock) can be a great way of bringing income into your business on a regular basis. You need to be careful about selling current stock (unless faulty) at these sales, as this can undermine your stockists and will also diminish the value of your brand. The e-commerce site *www.koodos.com* gives designers the opportunity to sell samples and excess stock online.

Additional material for this chapter supplied by Giacomo Corrado, Esq.
Corrado Montgomery, New York

Case Study: Karen Walker

Karen Walker set up her company, Karen Walker Limited, in 1989 when she was 19 and still at fashion college. She started with NZ$100 of her own money and designed and made a shirt which she sold in a local boutique. The reason she started on her own was because "there was no one around whose work I liked and who I wanted to work with."

The company has grown rapidly into a very successful global operation. Within four years they had their first stand-alone womenswear store, opening a second one in 1994. In 1995 they started to export into markets beyond New Zealand and, by 1998, they had stockists all over the world. In 2001 they expanded beyond fashion design and started their first interiors line—Karen Walker Paints—in partnership with leading paint manufacturer Resene. They have continued to expand their product range, launching a jewelry range in 2003 and a range of eyewear in 2005.

Karen is very clear about her market and about whom she likes to work with—"people like us." "We've never really worked based on location but based on personalities and as such we've developed a global niche brand. Our girl in Tokyo is the same as our girl in New York or Sydney or London." Karen has surrounded herself with people she likes and admires and this seems to be core to her success.

To add to this, Karen also attributes her success to making products that people like and to which they can relate. Next to product, she believes that placement is key, "because the environment tells so much about you and where you sit in the market." Initially the business was built entirely around wholesale, but now she has her own retail stores. These are boutique shops designed to create a relaxed, stylish, intimate, and fun shopping experience with lots to take in. She also licenses product, again subscribing to the "people like us" rule. "If we like the people and they get the idea within five minutes and have all the necessary skills and experience to make it work, and if it's a product that excited us, then we leap in."

To keep her product in the right environment, Karen also shows at New York Fashion Week. "It's about making it easy for your customer. Easy to see, understand, buy. And if it's all about making it easy

for your customer, you go where your customers are going to be when they're going to be there—in our case in New York during New York Fashion Week. That's not to say it's the only way, though. There are lots of ways to make it easy for your customer."

Karen ranks promotion and price below product and placement on the list of key contributors to success. "PR and marketing are, of course, an integral part of the fashion business but I knew intuitively right from the start that unless there's substance—an actual story to tell or product worth looking at—that you could have the best PR in the world and they wouldn't be able to do anything for you. The PR you create is only ever going to be as good as the product you sell." Price, she feels, will be set by the product, placement, and promotion.

Karen is driven by the fact that she likes what she does. She says she is "definitely still having fun, even when it's not fun. I get to structure my life how I want and I get the sense of satisfaction and pride (when it goes right) and there are a certain number of perks too." On the downside she says that "there's a lot of stuff that needs to be considered outside of just creating interesting design—there are a lot of distractions." But, if you want to be successful, you "must have the ability to understand business and be creative and responsible within business. You must also be a really fast learner because it's the kind of business where you have to run or stop. No walking."

Karen's aim is to make products that people both like and are able to relate to

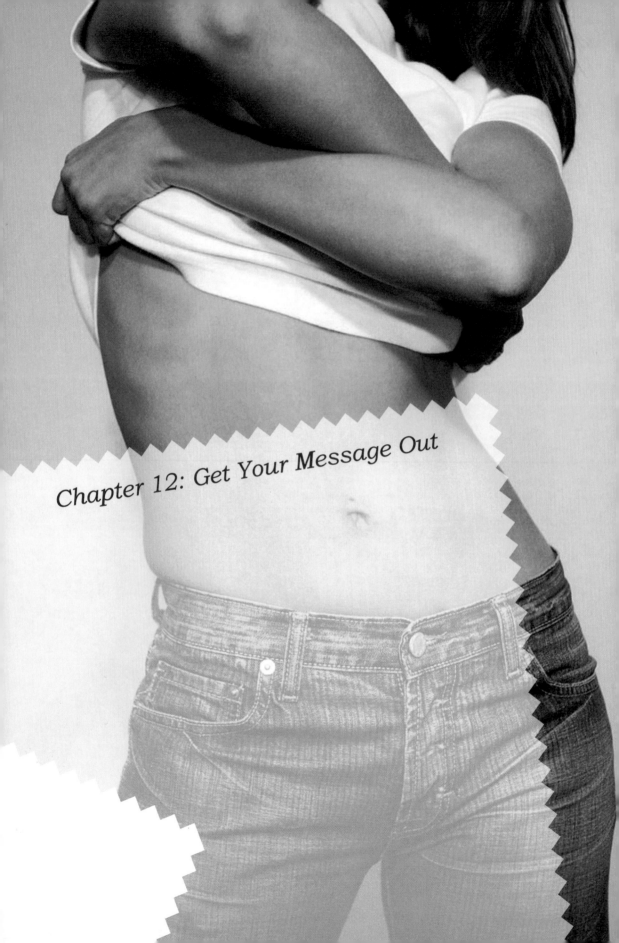

Chapter 12: Get Your Message Out

*Y*our new fashion label must convey a strong, identifiable message to which buyers, press, and consumers can relate. So do you want to be seen as young, sophisticated, edgy, luxurious, affordable, accessible, unique, quirky, pretty, sexy, trendy, conservative, functional, or exclusive?

Promotion is how you deliver your label's message to your target audience. It covers a wide range of activities: sales, advertising, publicity, special events, and websites. Your strategy should focus on getting people to buy your product, so you must pitch your activities correctly. If you are retailing, you will need to target the end consumer. If you are wholesaling, you will target both the end consumer and the retailers.

Look at Buying Behavior

An understanding of buying behavior will allow you to devise promotional activities that will influence the buying process.

Typical Consumer Buying Behavior
===

Identifies a need: *Often through press coverage, advertising, celebrity endorsement, or word of mouth.*

Looks for information: *From websites, advertising, and press. Can they find your label easily? Peer group recommendation is highly important. Visual aids, such as catalogs, posters, and so on are very useful.*

Checks out alternative suppliers and products: *Also known as "window shopping." You need to promote your product's uniqueness, and maximize packaging and displays. Sales personnel can have a huge influence. Make sure they are educated about your product. Third-party testimonial is still important. Value for money also becomes of major interest.*

Purchase decision: *Sales promotions and customer service come into their own.*

Use of the product: *Expensive purchases can lead to cognitive dissonance (see pages 103–4). You need to provide constant reassurance through good customer care, advertising, and third-party testimonials.*

Image by Malcolm Crews ===

Typical Business Buying Behavior

==

Identifies a need or problem: *Usually highlighted by advertising or press coverage (trade and consumer).*

Develops product specification: *Particular attention is paid to press releases, exhibitions, advertising, editorial comment, and relevant direct mail.*

Looks for products and suppliers: *Marketing material such as lookbooks, line sheets, and websites are of particular importance. Exhibitions/showrooms are also an invaluable source of information. At this point, pricing information begins to be seriously considered.*

Evaluates suppliers and products: *This is a good time to provide your potential customer with third-party testimonials. This can include references from other stores you sell to as well as relevant press. It is also the time when customers expect to see and feel the product to assess style and quality.*

Places an order: *Personal contact will help to close the order and increase its size.*

Evaluates supplier and product performance: *The larger the financial commitment the more reassurance is needed. Continued exposure to advertising and press coverage, together with phone calls and emails, will help to justify the decision to purchase.*

Reorders: *The first order placed should be seen not as the end of the process, but as the beginning of a long-term relationship.*

==

Promotional Materials

Some of your promotional materials will be specific to press and buyers, while others will target the consumer directly.

Lookbooks

Lookbooks introduce your product line or new season's collection to press and buyers. Catwalk designers usually take the images for their lookbooks from catwalk photographs. They are often presented as an A5 wire-bound glossy booklet, with 30 to 60 looks from the show, one photograph to a page.

The lookbook must have clear photographs of all your key products, with reference numbers, contact details, and website. If you include manufacturer's suggested retail prices (MSRPs) for each garment as well as a description of the product you can use the lookbook as a small sales catalog for consumers.

You could keep your printing costs down by selecting a few very strong images that give the essence of your collection and putting the rest on your website. However, busy journalists may just choose from the limited selection in your lookbook.

Lookbooks can come in varying shapes and sizes and are an essential tool for promoting your collection to press and buyers alike

Tips for Printing Lookbooks

===

Simon Assirati—*Managing Director, Solutions in Ink*

Images: *The printer will always produce a far better lookbook when using very high resolution images.*

"Fashion" printers focus on the garment rather than the model. The printer's job is to replicate the garments as closely as possible in printed format. This becomes increasingly technical when printing on different substrates of paper or board.

You can enhance the images, depending on the type of material used to print on— uncoated, coated matt, coated silk, or coated gloss finishes.

Before going to print, always ensure you have a digital proof from the printer as a final safety check. The color digital proof is 80 to 90 percent accurate in terms of color balance and is also good for checking text accuracy and image positioning.

Materials: *The majority of lookbooks are printed on a uniform boardweight throughout, such as 300gsm or 350gsm. This will also keep the cost down. Ask your printer to provide you with a free "mock-up" or unprinted dummy of your chosen lookbook.*

Enhancing the lookbook further can be done by using specialized finishes such as matt, silk, or gloss lamination on the paper or board; foil blocking in myriad colors; or debossing or embossing the material to give it a sunken or raised feel for a specific logo or piece of type.

Dimensions and binding are down to personal choice as well as cost. Printing, then creasing the board into panels, then folding them into a "pamphlet" type of finish is the most economical option. More flamboyant, costly lookbooks may be stitched or bound like a magazine.

Quantity: *Always print just enough, to avoid surplus stock the following season. Printers will quote for batches of 500 or 1,000 so you can see the price variations.*

===

Photography

Photography is especially important in a business like fashion where aesthetics are everything.

Developing a relationship with a photographer you trust is extremely important. Quite often you will be working to tight deadlines for shoots and you need to work with someone who can offer advice on what will work best and be most cost-effective. You may find the photographer can also help with things such as sourcing models, location, hair stylists, and make-up artists.

Planning a Fashion Shoot

===

Rikard Osterlund—*Freelance fashion photographer* (www.rikard.co.uk)

- -

Before you start, answer these simple questions. What is the purpose of the images? Who are they for? A lookbook (aimed at buyers) needs to show the details, prints, and silhouette of your designs, while an ad or editorial (aimed at consumers) needs to tell a story and create an atmosphere.

The key ingredients are: great clothes, a beautiful model, and a talented photographer.

Planning and preparation: *Have all your garments/designs ready (ironed and steamed), confirm with everyone in the team a few days before the shoot date, bring your inspiration, research, tear-sheets, and mood-boards. Hair and make-up take on average one to three hours. Make a call-sheet (all members of the team, contact details, addresses, times, and other info) and send it to everyone on the team.*

The team: *Photographer, model, location, lighting, stylist, hair stylist, make-up artist, props, and so on. Get your team together before you finalize your idea—they are the specialists.*

Photographer: *Find the one who can best illustrate your collection. Start by looking at photographers' portfolios—the AOP is a good place to start (www.image-folio.com), or find individual websites.*

Photography plays a very important role in the promotion of your collections. It is essential that you work with photographers who understand the message you are looking to deliver for your label and who can offer you the best possible shots to represent your product

Look for someone who suits your brand and collection (an amazing product photographer is perhaps not the ideal fashion photographer). Ask to meet up and have a look through the portfolio (every experienced photographer will have one). On the shoot the photographer is often the creative director so you need a good personal vibe.

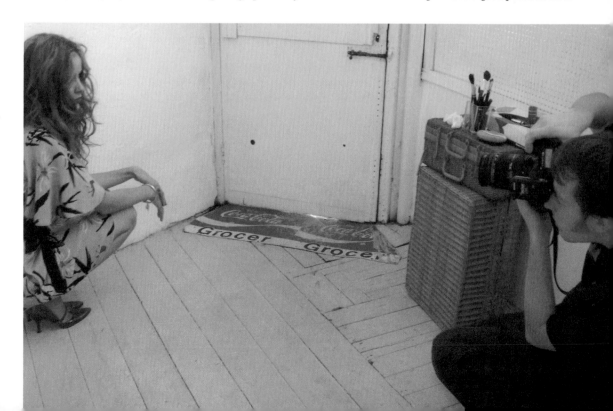

Charges/fees: *There is no set rate for commercial photography. A photographer's fee varies depending on the use of the images:*
- ✖ *Where the images will be displayed (packaging, website)*
- ✖ *How long they will be displayed for (a longer license will have a higher fee)*
- ✖ *Territory (UK, US, etc.).*

License to use/copyright: *The copyright in photographs always resides with the photographer.*

Story: *Contemporary fashion photography is more about the photograph than about the clothes. A series of images represents the dreams and desires of your clients, and it is driven by lighting, pose, and story. The series of images allows you to develop characters and introduce the clothes.*

Model: *Make sure a model's features match your collection. Contact the agencies beforehand, check prices and available models—the best ones are unlikely to do jobs on a small budget, so make sure you cast them, meet them, and see them in your clothes before you make the decision (that way you can check fittings). When you see a model wearing your clothes well it will click immediately.*

Book a second option in case of a no-show. Brief your model on the kind of person she or he is to become in the shoot (refer to your story).

The model's fee is based on similar parameters as the photographer's fee.

Ensure that the model signs a model release form, allowing you to use the images for your particular purpose. This is the contract (if you override this arrangement—for example, by hiring a model for a lookbook, then using the images for a campaign—you must inform the agent and pay the additional fees).

Location:
- ✖ *Natural light—realistic, soft*
- ✖ *Flash-lighting—sculptural, fantasy*
- ✖ *Light is the most important element, so make sure any indoor locations have big windows*
- ✖ *Use your contacts here—owners of many good locations know they are good and will charge you (try to avoid doing a trade for images, because if the location uses the images for promotion it is you and your photographer who will get in trouble)*
- ✖ *Props—find the right props to set off your collection.*

Hair stylist and make-up artist: *These specialists should add to your story, and the character of the model. Arrange a meeting, view portfolios, and see if they are confident about working on your shoot.*

After the shoot: *Some digital photographers will give the client a CD with preview images directly after the shoot, while others may post a selection of images on a website. Once the images have been selected, they will be taken through the digital workflow (digital version of film-processing). Any professional fashion images are then retouched. Retouching is expensive so make sure you have limited your selection.*

Make sure you tell the photographer what you need the images for (website or posters, etc.) as the images will be set up differently depending on the output.

==

Line Sheets

A line sheet is a sales sheet used for wholesale purposes, providing information on all products or seasonal styles. It is usually sent out to buyers with the lookbook. It should include:

✖ Logo
✖ Season (fall/winter; spring/summer)
✖ Styles (usually line drawings but sometimes photographs)
✖ Style names
✖ Style numbers
✖ Color and fabric information.

On the back page include:
✖ Delivery dates and order cut-off dates
✖ Order minimums
✖ Sales agent's contact information.

Additional information:
✖ Swatch card.

STORY	STYLE NAME	STYLE NO.	COLOR NAME	UPPER	US W/S (X 2.6)	US MSRP	IMAGE
Figure of eight	TABITHA	LG2447	Black	Patent leather	$75.00	$195.00	
Figure of eight	TESSA	LG2461	Plum	Leather	$71.15	$185.00	
Figure of eight	RENE	LG2444	Black Black stripes Raspberry	Textile	$75.00	$195.00	
Figure of eight	SUNNY	LG2442	Black Raspberry	Patent leather	$67.50	$175.00	
Figure of eight	ISABELLA	LG2420	Plum	Leather	$61.55	$160.00	
Figure of eight	ISABELLA	LG2421	Black stripes	Textile	$61.55	$160.00	
Figure of eight	FIFI	LG2438	Plum Black Cream	Patent leather	$65.50	$170.00	
Figure of eight	FIFI	LG2439	Bronze	Leather	$65.50	$170.00	
Figure of eight	FIFI	LG2478	Raspberry	Suede	$65.50	$170.00	
Figure of eight	FREDERICA	LG2449	Plum Bronze Raspberry	Leather	$52.00	$135.00	
Figure of eight	FREDERICA	LG2450	Black Cream	Patent leather	$52.00	$135.00	

Line sheets are used for sales purposes and provide the buyer with the key information needed to place an order

Stationery

You will need business cards, letterheads, and compliment (comp) slips, designed to reinforce your label's image.

Swing Tickets

Stores will expect you to attach swing tickets to your products for retail purposes. It can also look professional to have swing tickets (with the wholesale price) when wholesaling.

Labels

The customer looks to the label of a garment to identify the brand and gauge the quality of the product. You can have your label custom-made by a manufacturer to make it unique.

You will also need care labels. These should include fabric information, care advice, and other special instructions. They communicate the size of the garment and the place of origin (laws on place of origin details vary from country to country).

When developing your swing tickets it is important to carry through the brand image you are looking to project. Iconic Japanese streetwear label A Bathing Ape has cleverly incorporated its logo into a camouflage design to reinforce its brand message

Websites

Much as a shop window should entice a customer into the store, your website should entice people into your brand.

Websites are often the first point of contact for press, buyers, and consumers looking for information on your label and therefore need to project your message clearly.

Tips for Planning a Website

===

1   *Select a color scheme and stick to it.*

2   *Templates can be a cheap and effective way of developing your site. See www.web4business.com.au; www.templates.bigwebmaster.com/fashion/; www.webuildpages.com/web-design/fashion-website-templates.htm; www.website-templates-resale-rights.com; www.templatemonster.com; www.templatesbox.com.*

3   *Make navigation around the site as easy as possible.*

4   *Don't get carried away with special effects.*

5   *Make sure fonts can be easily read against backgrounds.*

6   *Content is king.*

===

Social Media

Social media is the commonly used term to describe interactive content that is developed using web-based technologies. The key component is the interactive nature, which allows people to share their opinions, insights, and even content with other web users. You are bringing other people into the conversation rather than just telling them about what is going on. For a fashion label, this means engaging with your consumer, quite often inviting them behind the scenes of your business. The growth of the use of social media among individuals took place rapidly and continues to expand. The adoption of social media by business was a little slower, with many organizations wary of letting the consumer behind the scenes for fear of damaging their well-crafted brand image. Whereas traditional models of communication such as advertising allow the promoter to control content and output, minimizing the risk of their message being misinterpreted or diluted, social media begins a dialog that is ongoing and constantly shaping the way you and your business are perceived. However, brands are turning to social media to deliver their messages more than ever. Richard Spalding, CEO of Diffusion Media, a socially focused agency specializing in tactical online marketing for blue-chip brand Agent Provocateur, says, "Agent Provocateur have invested heavily in social media over 2010/11 and there is evidence to suggest that the payoff is significant in terms of online sales increase." He also explains that for many brands "it is often hard to measure efficacy of social media." It is an "always on" channel, which is "very cost-effective when you get it right" but it can lead to "indifference when you get it wrong." Ultimately, though, he believes that in this day and age "failing to drive a social media strategy for any new business would be fatal." This is a sentiment backed up by Amelia Gregory, Publisher of *Amelia's Magazine* and social media maven: "It's vital that emerging fashion designers embrace social media because it's an incredibly fluid and wide-reaching way to engage press and potential buyers, both retail and individual."

The content used for social media tends to fall into one of four categories: text, image, audio, or video. Different social media platforms lend themselves to different types of content. Some of the most relevant types of platform for fashion start-ups include:

✖ *Social networking:* Create a personal profile or a company page then chat and share information, videos, photos, and audio with others. E.g. Facebook, MySpace, Bebo.

✖ *Presence applications:* Create micro-blog-like posts stating your current activity, thought, or point of interest. E.g. Twitter.

✖ *Video sharing:* Upload and share your videos or even create your own brand channel. E.g. YouTube.

✖ *Photo sharing:* Upload pictures and images to be viewed by an online community of your choosing. E.g. Flickr.

✖ *Wikis:* Create, edit, and share information about a brand, person, subject, or topic. E.g. Wikipedia.

Part of the challenge for a small start-up is managing your social media strategy and finding the time both to develop content and maximize its exposure. While social media can be a cost-effective way to promote your label there is no doubt that the rewards are in line with the amount of time you put in. It is therefore essential to decide early on what your strategy is going to be and to focus on those media that best suit your business.

Tips for Maximizing Exposure of Your Social Media Content

===

Richard Spalding—*CEO of Diffusion Media*

— —

Use Facebook: *Set up a Facebook page and put all your content, pictures, videos, (link from a YouTube Channel) etc. on it. Facebook is where your audience are. Don't expect people to visit a blog, they want to "socialize" where their friends are. Facebook is highly optimized for search, so if people want to find you or your product, they will find you a lot more easily here.*

Build a following: *If you've got something interesting to say, people will naturally descend on your Facebook page and "like" it. Design the page with as much enthusiasm as you would your business. You'll get noticed.*

Make video and promote it: *Video is cheap to make; HD now comes on an iPhone. Create lots of short video content and send it around, host it all on your Facebook page and get your friends to "like" it and comment on it.*

Set up a YouTube channel: *Design the background like your Facebook page, place all your video content on here and then subscribe to and befriend everyone you can on YouTube who may like your work. Then every time you make a video, you can send it to all of your friends and subscribers.*

Focus: *Use just Facebook and YouTube as your social "outlet." Don't try and run a YouTube channel, Facebook page, Twitter feed, and a blog. Keep it simple and focus on where the audience is.*

Blog: *There are hundreds of online designers and geeks who can design and help you build these channels. They are very simple to maintain once set up.*

===

When starting out in social media it is important to find your voice and the voice of your label. Who are you and how do you want to be perceived? How much of the reality of running your business are you willing to share? Some designers report their day-to-day activities, good or bad, to help develop a personal dialog with their followers, while other labels maintain a more professional "brand" dialog. The voice needs to suit the situation, as Amelia Gregory states when talking about Twitter. "It's an incredibly egalitarian way of communicating because it allows users to network across hierarchies, but you should still be aware of subtle boundaries. For example, always consider the way in which you approach someone you might want to do business with, because the first contact you make will be crucial in determining how they view your brand."

Events

Exhibitions

Exhibitions are a great place to meet trade and consumer press and promote your name and brand, so have a press pack (see page 170) available. Consumer shows also give your label direct exposure to the public.

Networking Events

People, especially the right people, need to know about you. Official networking events for small business owners and the fashion industry take place all the time so keep an eye out for any press announcements of such events.

Getting out and about to parties is also a great way of spreading your name around. Getting invited to the right parties where the fashionistas hang out is all about befriending the event organizers. The greater your label's reputation, the more invites you will receive.

Catwalks

The catwalk is the designer's one opportunity each season to invite the world's press and buyers to see the latest creations and gain as much exposure as possible.

Catwalks are often an exciting way for fashion labels to promote their latest collections and, depending on the market you are looking to target, may take place either during the major fashion weeks around the world or at consumer shows direct to the public

Catwalk Checklist

===

Venue
Is the venue large enough, centrally located, and visually suitable for your brand? Can it accommodate a catwalk, seating for guests, and a large backstage area?

Risk assessment/insurance
You will need to check that the venue has public liability insurance. If producing the show yourself you will need public liability and employer liability insurance.

Catwalk/runway
A raised catwalk allows a large audience to get a good look at the collection from the top of the model's head to the shoes on her feet. A floor-level runway area can work just as well.

Music
The music you choose should help create the story your collection is trying to tell the audience. You will need a performing rights license. If you're using a DJ, check with him/her to see if they have a license. If not, you'll need to apply for a one-day permit.

Personnel
Backstage you will need a team of dressers. Students from fashion colleges are happy to help out in this capacity. They must be briefed individually on the outfits they are in charge of—any detailing of position or placement needs to be explained.

Try to have someone to look after front-of-house, including guests.

Models
Use reputable model agencies. The number and reputation of your models will depend on the size of your budget. You will need to hold a casting—look through the models' portfolios and get them to walk up and down to make sure they are suitable for the look of your show. Don't take too much time with each. Take a picture of those you like in order to remember them. Once you have made your selection call the agencies to book the models. If there are a number of shows on at the same time they will give you an option. As the show gets closer they will confirm. You will need to give a call time for the models to arrive on the day. It is quite common during a busy period to have only four hours before the show— other shows may run late and so will your models. Make sure there are refreshments for the models—you want them to look and feel their best.

You must negotiate with the agency for usage. Most fees only include the catwalk show; if you want to use images from the show for lookbooks, websites, or advertising, you will need to pay more.

Photographer
Book a catwalk photographer to take photos to send out to press contacts who didn't manage to come along. Try to get one with good press contacts and who has experience of taking catwalk pictures. See www.vogue.com or www.style.com for the type of shots you should be looking for.

Lighting
Get professional help. It needn't be expensive but you need to have the right lighting for the photography.

Hair and make-up

You will need a dedicated hair and make-up team. They might need 30 to 60 minutes per model. Fashion colleges or hair salons can be a good place to find people to work for nothing—as long as they get a mention. You may be able to get sponsorship (see below).

Invitations

These should be sent out at least four weeks in advance of your catwalk show (less if you are showing during an official fashion week and your name has been put on a schedule). Invitations should be ready to go to print at least six weeks in advance. Do a call-around closer to the show to gauge numbers and start to devise a seating plan. It is common to see press seated on one side and buyers, celebrities, and VIPs on the other.

Compère

If you are organizing a catwalk show for consumers to watch rather than trade buyers and press it can be a good idea to have a compère introducing the show— someone with confidence and a good sense of humor. You may want to produce a script to make sure all the sponsors get a mention and the important points about your collection are put across.

Credit sheet and press release

A credit sheet with acknowledgments, sponsors' logos, and an at-show press release (with your contact details) about the collection should be placed on each seat.

Press and media

A month before the show, send out a press release and follow up with a phone call. Two weeks beforehand send out another press release and follow up with another phone call. You will need to give the press an angle. Catwalk shows are great visual stories and can generate regional and national TV coverage.

===

Press Days

Labels that don't show on the catwalk often arrange a day for the press to come and view the collection in person in a hotel in a central location, or in the designer's studio. As an unknown label you will need to work hard to make sure the press attend—you may find that taking the collection to the press is more effective in the early days.

Sponsorship/Collaborations

Sponsorship of catwalk shows is very common. Beauty and lifestyle giants such as L'Oréal will often get involved with the hair and make-up and can send out the message that you are working with some of the industry's biggest and best brands.

Brands like Mizani look to work with designers and shows that complement their own brand ethos and promote their products to a wider audience

Nzinga Russell for Mizani says:

"Mizani is a premium haircare range specifically formulated for the hair and scalp of excessively curly hair textures. As an exclusive, salon-only, professional brand we are committed to the stylist and part of this commitment is our passion for fashion and creativity. This is why Kulture 2 Couture was perfect for us.

"As a growing brand we are always looking for opportunities to raise our profile as well as inspire creativity. K2C fulfilled both of these needs as it allowed us to strengthen our link with fashion. Supporting up-and-coming talent is often one of the most rewarding and exciting ways of doing this. It's also always good to get involved with an initiative early on in its development as you can then create real synergy and collaboration between the two brands.

"Hair and fashion are inextricably linked so not only did the relationship make great commercial sense for us, it was something we were fundamentally passionate about which made for a great pairing."

Designers can often also be asked to take part in collaborative projects. A make-up brand may ask a designer to come up with a limited edition make-up bag. A cell phone company may want a phone case for promotional purposes. This can be a great way for your label to gain wider recognition and a welcome source of income. While it is often the marketing managers who approach the designers, don't be afraid to put a pitch together if you think you have a great idea that would tie in brilliantly with another company's marketing strategy.

Caroline Mackay, Brand Manager for Knomo:

"As a new tech-relevant accessories brand, we wanted to up the ante in the fashion stakes and really make a splash with the fashion press. We were put in touch with fashion event OnlOff and came across the beautiful designs of fashion label Belle & Bunty. Together we hit upon the idea of putting one of their striking prints across our best-selling 'Cholet' women's bag. We certainly

got what we hoped for—the bags were a huge hit with customers and were
featured in *Marie Claire* and *Grazia*; we were only sorry we didn't produce more
of them!"

Public Relations

PR is crucial in getting your fashion label's message out and is a much more
cost-effective medium than advertising. It is well suited to the fashion industry
because there is always something new to write about.

What's Your Story?

You need to understand what it is the fashion press want to cover. Examine
how and why magazines put together the fashion pages as they do.

Niki Turner, PR and Marketing Manager for Kurt Geiger:

"Understand the publication you are pitching to. Ensure you demonstrate
knowledge of their pages and don't ever just do a blanket pitch for a story. Find
an angle to suit each publication and always make sure you only get in contact
with a story that is relevant and will be of interest. Remember, a journalist
receives hundreds of press releases a week so be imaginative and work out
the best approach to get their attention without being detrimental to your
brand. The most common complaint I hear from fashion journalists is the
amount of rubbish they get sent with no forethought into what their page/
column is about. Journalists are keen to hear about stories that have a hook
and are newsworthy such as collaborations, charity link-ups, and celebrity."

Tips for Getting Press Coverage

==

✖ **Play reporter:** *Think like the journalist. What is it they want to cover for their readership? What topics or products are of interest? What angles will they find fresh and provocative?*

✖ **Tailored pitches:** *When you deliver a pitch, you're tailoring an idea for a single reporter. You're saying, "I think you'll be interested in this idea because...."*

✖ **Think long term:** *Get to know the journalists so that even if the reporter doesn't take you up on your offer this time, you can be confident your next pitch will be read. It's all about relationships.*

==

Press Pack

When approaching the media you should have a press pack containing all the material needed to cover your story. A basic pack should include:

✖ History and overview
✖ Designer's biography
✖ Lookbook
✖ Press release
✖ Contact details.

The label's history and the designer's biography will need constant updating, while your lookbook will need to be reprinted seasonally to reflect your new product range. Journalists and stylists will go through the lookbooks for key pieces to shoot for their publication.

Press releases should be tailored to the specific story or announcement. Typical stories that might warrant a release include: launch of your new collection, new major distribution outlets for your product, celebrity tie-ins.

Format for a Typical Press Release

==

FOR IMMEDIATE RELEASE
These words should appear in the upper left-hand margin in capital letters.

Headline
A sentence that gives the essence of what the press release is about. Articles, prepositions, and conjunctions of three letters or fewer should be lowercase.

Dateline
The city from which your press release is issued and the date you are mailing your release.

Lead paragraph
A strong introductory paragraph should grab the reader's attention and should contain the information most relevant to your message, such as the five W's (who, what, when, where, why). It should summarize the press release and include a hook to get your audience interested in reading more.

Body
This is where your message should fully develop. Many companies choose to use a strategy called the inverted pyramid, which is written with the most important information and quotes first.

Boilerplate
Your press release should end with a short paragraph that describes your label, products, service, and a short history.

Contact details
Name, phone number, email address, and website.

==

Your press pack will not guarantee coverage. PR is about developing relationships with the media, and you will need to pick up the phone and talk directly with the journalists responsible for the particular column you are looking to get into. When you call you need to know exactly what you are going to say and that you are talking to the right person. Once the relationship has been established you will find that journalists start coming to you with call-ins (see below) for shoots and editorials. This is when you know the relationship is working.

==

TASK

Draw up a hotlist of 20 journalists or editors
Identify the publications whose readerships best match your target customer. Go through each publication and make a list of the key journalists and the pages they are responsible for. Narrow them down to the key 20 journalists. These will be the focus of your PR activities.

==

Call-Ins

A call-in is when a journalist or stylist requests your product for a still life or editorial shoot they are doing. They will usually say they are interested in particular pieces of your collection that they have seen in your lookbook. If you have only a few images in your lookbook this could be the time to point them in the direction of extra images on your website. The more they choose, the greater the likelihood there is of something being shot for their story.

Responsibility for getting your product to the journalist or stylist can differ depending on the publication or program calling in the pieces. Major publications and TV shows will often arrange for a courier at their expense. They will also be responsible for the return delivery. This obviously depends on whether you are located near the major media outlets. At other times you may be responsible for delivering your collection. Don't be afraid to ask if they can arrange for a pick-up. If you are based away from the main media outlets, you may need to look for representation with a PR agency based close to the key publications. They will hold on to your most pressworthy samples for call-ins and will take over the responsibility for all your press enquiries.

Keeping track

Once a call-in has come through make a record of exactly what is being sent out, when, and to whom, and the shoot date. Keep one copy and put one in the package (with your contact details) with the call-in. Include a disclaimer that all damaged or unreturned pieces will be charged at full price. The press can call in hundreds of pieces a day, all of which will go through their fashion cupboard, and things can go astray. You want to get your pieces back as soon as they have been shot to make sure you are ready for the next time they are called in.

Press Book and Show Cards

Just because your product gets called in doesn't mean it will actually make the final publication or program. If your product is being featured in a magazine, you will usually receive a phone call requesting a recommended retail price and a stockist's address or phone number. Once you know your product has been covered find out which edition it will be featured in. Buy a copy to add to your press book. It is a great tool for showing buyers, consumers, and potential investors about the buzz your label is creating. You can also put press coverage on your website.

For really great pieces of press, you can order show cards from the publication, for a fee. Feature your show cards prominently at trade exhibitions to show potential buyers that you are a label that is being talked about. You can also get a few extra cards for any key stockists that have bought the piece featured to display.

Show cards are a great way of letting buyers and customers know the press you have achieved and can help to sell your product

Dressing Celebrities

Getting your product endorsed by the right celebrity can do wonders for your fashion label. However, the message you send is inextricably linked with the message the celebrity sends out. If you are producing expensive red-carpet dresses this can be great if the celebrity is a suave and sophisticated Hollywood A-lister, but not so great if the celebrity is regarded as a cheap and tacky D-lister.

The key to dressing celebrities is building a relationship with their stylists. Although the celebrity will ultimately choose what they think suits them best they can be heavily influenced by their stylists. The more visible your fashion label, the more likely it is that a fashion stylist will contact you to request product. However, services such as Red Pages (*www.theredpages.co.uk*) offer access to contact details for celebrities all over the world for a monthly fee. Quite often the contact is the agent representing the celebrity. It is then up to you to contact them. Usually they will write back and point you in the direction of the stylist.

Oz and Kat Aalam from London boutique Damsel say:

"The most helpful thing to us from a selling point of view is magazine features or celebrity coverage."

In House v Agency

If the thought of cold calling journalists turns you into a quivering wreck it then may be best to find someone to do your PR, either in house or through a reputable agency specializing in fashion PR.

Pros and Cons

==

In House

Advantages:

✘ *Has onsite access to other key internal functions*
✘ *Can deal quickly and effectively with range of external queries*
✘ *Understands the brand's market position/history in depth*
✘ *Gives 100 percent effort and attention to your label.*

Disadvantage:

✘ *Is a fixed cost to your business (although can be part-time).*

Agency

Advantages:

✘ *Specialist team with resources (writers and production)*
✘ *Objectivity may produce fresh ideas and approach*
✘ *Wider range of contacts/experience*
✘ *Variable cost to your business.*

Disadvantage:

✘ *Focus may be on bigger clients.*

==

PR agencies usually work on a monthly retainer basis and costs can vary from $750 a month for a small agency taking on a start-up to $15,000+ for the top agencies working with more established brands. If you are working to a very tight budget, spend on sales rather than a PR agency, which is a long-term investment. There are hundreds of fashion labels in existence that you will never have heard of, as they do not have a high media profile, but are making very nice money for themselves. They have focused on developing a strong customer base through marketing and sales activities rather than chasing the press. All the hype in the world won't make your business a success if your product disappoints your customers.

Case Study: Soulland

Danish designer Silas Adler launched his fashion label Soulland in 2002 at the age of 17, with no formal training in fashion. He admits he jumped in at the deep end. "I started young and with no experience. I did not have a plan or anything like that in the beginning. I just jumped into it. I actually started the company with some friends from my high school. We were into skateboarding and didn't go to school much. One morning I woke up and thought to myself, why go to school when I can start a clothing company? So I did."

In the beginning they produced T-shirts, selling them to friends and small skateboard stores. His friends soon got bored and returned to school, but Silas kept going. "When I think back now I don't know why I did what I did. Everything was new and I didn't have any experience, but I learned all the time. I guess you can say I created my own school."

For the first couple of years Silas had different jobs on the side. He also did an internship and worked for fashion retailer WoodWood. "At some point I thought to myself; okay if you are going do this you have to do it 100 percent," so he quit everything and started to work full time, creating a ready-to-wear collection which included ten different styles.

His mother helped him formalize the business, but in 2007 he found a business partner, Jacob Kampp Berliner. Jacob had experience of developing a jewelry label in Denmark, loved the Soulland ethos, and was keen to invest some money into the business. Initially only an investor, in 2009 Jacob became a full time member of staff and runs the company day to day along with Silas.

Soulland now offers two seasonal full range menswear collections a year. Silas says, "you need to have a product that is adding something extra special to the market" and the "product has to be matched by the pricing strategy so that the target consumer will buy." Wholesale has been the main focus for the business in the early years, but recently they have opened their first retail space, although Silas admits that it is too early to decide whether this is the direction they will move in the future.

Production was initially taken care of locally, but as the range developed they have moved most of the production to Portugal. Their hat collection is still produced locally in Copenhagen and promotes

traditional artisan techniques as part of its added value. For Silas "production is by far the most frustrating part of running the business."

PR has always been undertaken in house and has been essential in building the awareness of Soulland, as has networking. As a key member of the skateboard community Silas is friends with people from different countries and cultures because "skateboarding is something we have in common" and he believes fashion can be similar. "It's very important to be open in the way you network, you never know where the people you meet along the way will end up." As part of their PR strategy Soulland put on a seasonal catwalk show as soon as they produced their first full collection. Even though no other menswear brand was showcasing in Copenhagen at the time "it made sense for us" and as a result "we are now one of the most popular shows during Copenhagen fashion week."

For Silas the opportunity to develop his own creative output is great and he thoroughly enjoys being his own boss. Watching his ideas grow into something that can actually pay the bills is also a great reward. "Working with my team and the feeling of lifting this ship together" are constant sources of inspiration while "always being better and learning is an important motivator for me." While he and his team work extremely hard to develop the business he also says, "We have a lot of fun!" Silas believes fashion entrepreneurs "need to be very flexible and ready to navigate in alternative ways at all times as two days are never the same." He also says it's important to "keep being humble" as "you are only as good as your last design." Silas advises someone setting up their business "four times out of five think before you act, one time out of five act before you think, and learn from it."

Soulland has grown from selling just T-shirts to become one of Denmark's top emerging menswear brands

I AM LOCKED IN A VERY EXPENSIVE SUIT

Chapter 13: Finance

*T*he financial side of setting up a fashion label is quite often the area that most aspiring fashion entrepreneurs decide to tackle last. However, it's better to sort out the financial aspects of your business right from the outset. As Caroline Charles states: "Try not to separate the design and marketing process from the finance side—the sooner you can embrace them all as part of the creative process the greater success and more fun you will have." This chapter will guide you through the steps you need to take to get your business off the ground and raise it to a sustainable level. This will include the cost of office space, manufacturing, marketing, office equipment, and contingency.

Projecting Your Start-Up Costs

Formal attire by Pose London

Projecting your start-up costs often proves tricky for new fashion labels. The box below shows the main initial expenses and ongoing expenses that you will typically encounter. By researching the areas listed you should be able to come up with a good estimate for each area. Include your reasonable salary expectations even if at first you will be unable to draw a salary. With only a limited pot of money available you must prioritize your costs.

Start-Up Costs

Initial Expenses	Ongoing Expenses
Incorporating	Rent or mortgage
Legal and accounting	Utilities
Office/studio costs including: rent, security deposit or property purchase, furniture, equipment	Staff payroll/your salary
Research including: production, fabric/trim suppliers, exhibitions, customer base	Production
Travel	Marketing/sales/advertising
Marketing materials: business cards, letterheads, websites, etc.	Travel
First samples	Insurance
	Taxes
	Debt repayment
	Working capital

Projecting Income

Projecting income can be much harder than projecting expenses. Most fashion start-ups will not have a starting point from which to predict revenue. You will have to make assumptions based on research into your given market. After your first 12 months of trading you will at least have the previous year's figures to go on.

Start by predicting the number of stores you aim to sell to in your first season. Initial orders from boutiques might range from just $1,000 to $2,000—the buyers will want to see how well your product will sell. If you aim to sell to chain retailers you may find that you can sell significantly larger numbers, ranging from the hundreds to thousands of dollars per order, with one account producing tens of thousands of dollars of revenue.

When projecting income in the early stages, look at your projected income and expenses and ask "What if?" What if you only make half the sales you have projected? What if you only make a quarter? What if you make no first season sales? These are the scenarios that might drastically affect your business from the very outset.

Although your personal finances may cover most of your start-up costs, you might need a cash injection to pay for production in your first season. By projecting your capital requirements early, you will be in a position to start a dialog with your bank in time for an overdraft to be in place as and when needed.

Check Out Sources of Funding

Thoroughly research the finance available to you and make sure you understand the terms and conditions of any loan. Have your accountant look over the possibilities, which might include:
* Personal savings
* Friends and relatives
* Banks and credit unions
* Grants/local governmental agencies
* Angel financing/venture capital firms.

Personal Savings

If the amount needed to set up the label is relatively small, you may be able to cover it from your personal finances. You retain control by not relying on hand-outs from others who may want to have some say in the running of things. The obvious downside is that it's your money you're risking!

Friends and Relatives

Borrowing money from friends and relatives is quite often an emotional choice and can put a strain on relationships if the lending terms are not laid out in full or adhered to. Write down the terms under which the money is being lent, and when and under what circumstances repayment is due.

Banks and Credit Unions

Most banks and credit unions will provide a loan or an overdraft if you can show that your business proposal is sound and you are credit worthy. You should be aware that banks require formal loan applications, business plans, and financial projections. They are then subject to analytical scrutiny, underwriting, and credit checks.

Ideally loans should be used to buy fixed assets, such as sewing machines and computers, for start-up capital, and for other cases where the amount of money you need is fixed. It is quite common for a loan guarantee to be required.

An overdraft is often used to help your business with its day-to-day cash flow, including working capital, and ongoing expenses. Expenses are best funded from the cash received from your sales, but where a shortfall may arise in the short term it is possible to use an overdraft as back-up.

Check out any lender before committing. You should compare interest rates of the various lenders to see how competitive they are by going to a site called *www.bandrate.com.*

Remember:

Most lenders will require you to:
- ✖ *Match their loan from your own resources*
- ✖ *Have a fall-back option if it all goes wrong*
- ✖ *Offer something as security—you should take professional advice before entering a secured loan agreement*
- ✖ *Keep them regularly informed of your progress, particularly any changes or problems*
- ✖ *Have a comprehensive business plan.*

Grants and Local Governmental Agencies

Grants are given to businesses or individuals for a specified purpose or project. As long as you stick to any conditions stipulated by the grant, you will not have to repay it or give up ownership of your business. However, grants usually cover only part of the total costs—it is common for you to have to match funds. Grants that apply to your specific needs can take a lot of research to find and even more paperwork to achieve. Just make sure that the time spent trying to obtain the grant isn't costing your business more than the amount of the grant.

It is certainly well worth keeping an eye out for grant information, but just be prepared to fill in the paperwork. The SBA (*www.sba.gov*) site offers links and a search facility for grants and financial support from various government sponsored agencies.

Angel Financing and Venture Capital Firms

Angel financing is provided by wealthy private investors who take equity stakes in small, high-risk firms.

They will often provide their own business expertise to make sure their investment has the best chance of success. Although more likely to invest in a business that has a successful track record, some prefer to spread their wealth in smaller investment amounts to young entrepreneurs with a great business plan. Small fashion start-ups often find their angels through word of mouth and introductions from friends and family. SCORE—Counselors to America's Small Business (*www.score.org*)—offers advice and tips.

On a much larger scale, venture capital firms usually help expanding businesses grow in exchange for equity or partial ownership. The fashion industry is a bad risk for venture capital as it is not considered to have high or quick returns.

Once you have decided on the right route you must draw up a financial plan that will make sense to both you and your prospective lender.

Make an Offer that Can't Be Refused

Your business plan must be succinct and explain as clearly as possible exactly what you intend to do. It should outline the nature and type of your business, any personal investment and how that will be used to meet specific goals, timelines, financial objectives, analysis of your competition, and how your business will fit in the marketplace. It should be watertight and convince prospective lenders that you and your business are a good investment. There are many organizations that you can go to for advice on writing your business plan and your local SBA or SCORE should be able to point you in the right direction. Ask if they know of anyone with specialist knowledge of the fashion industry.

Elements of a Business Plan

==

1 Cover sheet

2 Statement of purpose

3 Table of contents

I. The business
✖ *Description of business*
✖ *Marketing*
✖ *Competition*
✖ *Operating procedures*
✖ *Personnel*
✖ *Business insurance*
✖ *SWOT analysis*

II. Financial data
✖ *Loan applications*
✖ *Capital equipment and supply list*
✖ *Balance sheet*
✖ *Break-even analysis*
✖ *Profit and loss statements—detail by month, for first three years (include assumptions upon which projections were based—inflation, growth, currency rates, if applicable)*
✖ *Month-by-month cash flow*

III. Supporting documents
✖ *Tax returns of principals for last three years*
✖ *Personal financial statement (all banks have these forms)*
✖ *Copy of proposed lease or purchase agreement for building space*
✖ *Copies of licenses and other legal documents*
✖ *Copies of resumes of all principals*
✖ *Copies of letters of intent from suppliers, etc.*

==

 ## Tips for Preparing a Business Plan

✖ *Find business plan templates on the internet. One is included with the online resources for this book; download it at www.laurenceking.com.*
✖ *Spell out strategies on how you intend to handle unforeseen events.*
✖ *Spell out the strengths and weaknesses of your management team.*
✖ *Include at least a monthly one-year cash flow projection.*
✖ *Package your business plan in an attractive kit as a selling tool.*
✖ *Submit your business plan to experts in your intended business for their advice.*
✖ *Freely and frequently modify your business plans to account for changing conditions after start-up, but always keep the original and a summary of why changes are occurring.*

==

Validate Your Projections

Cash flow projections illustrating both the viability of your start-up and your ability to repay any loans will probably be asked for. Keep the figures realistic and back them up with facts that validate your estimates and projections. Ask your accountant to look over the numbers, but remember that you will need to be able to explain to any lenders what the figures mean and what the consequences of not hitting targets will be.

Practice Makes Perfect

In order to access start-up financing you will need to present your ideas at some point. Take time to think your pitch through and practice in front of other people who can provide constructive feedback. You need to be prepared for all kinds of questions about your business concept including product, price, market, and your own personal background.

Tips for Pitching to Potential Investors

===

Excite
Express passion about your company. Try to create a buzz if you want them to remember you.

Keep it short
Stick to the basics. Don't overwhelm them with information.

Engage the audience
Encourage questions and provoke discussion by asking your own questions about the investors, their interests, and past ventures.

Avoid templates
Tailor your pitch to fit the needs of your company and the investors to whom you are presenting.

Be truthful
Don't try to be more than you are or can be just to impress the investors.

Be clear, detailed, and concise
Make sure that you keep the language simple and resist the urge to use jargon. Talk about your fashion business's unique points, your product, customers, and what market void you are looking to fill and how you are going to fill it. Introduce your team, their relevant qualifications, and the role that they will play. Outline your business model and map out your financial projections (up to five years), requirements, and milestones.

Be realistic
Show that you have ambitious plans for your fashion business but don't get carried away. Investors will want to see you have a grip on the market and reality.

Be in control
Remember that investment is a two-way relationship. You are looking for the right investors as much as they are looking for the right investment. Be confident and in control.

Be prepared
You need to be prepared for a thorough investigation of your projections and your team capabilities.

===

Questions, Questions, Questions

Borrowing money is a big step. Get all the information you need about potential lenders' processes and loan expectations. Speak with friends and relatives about lenders they have used and involve your accountant in the process.

Find a Good Accountant

A good accountant can save you a lot of money and need not be expensive.

To find a good and reliable accountant you can start by asking for references from friends and business associates. You can also contact the AICPA (American Institute of Certified Public Accountants—*www.aicpa.com*) or your local State Society of CPAs.

How to Cost Your Product

If you're to sell at a profit, you need to have calculated the cost correctly. Although many companies are good at calculating the direct costs of things such as fabric, the other components (thread, fastening, trims, labels, freight, and labor) are often not as well costed.

Some designers simply add from 30 to 40 percent to the final product cost to include overheads, also known as indirect costs, before adding their profit margin. While this can make costing easier it can make it more difficult to cut costs.

A useful tool in calculating the true cost of your product is the Cost of Goods spreadsheet (see page 191). The headings in your spreadsheet will depend on the product you are making, but the template should give you an idea of the costs you should be factoring in. Most costs will be straightforward. Others will need to be calculated before being entered. You may pay $160 to have a dress pattern cut and graded. If you anticipate selling only one dress then you will have to factor in the full $160. However, if you believe you will sell 20, the cost per dress will be $160 ÷ 20 = $8. If you will reuse this pattern on a seasonal basis, the actual cost for each garment may be minimal.

By working through the spreadsheet you can develop wholesale and retail price points for your product. This will depend on the mark-up you decide to work from. Designer labels often mark up between two and three times, or 100 to 200 percent. With a mark-up of three, roughly one third covers the costs, one third covers the overheads, and the final third is profit.

However, many designers start by determining how much their product should be retailing for—the perceived value. If you start from this you can then divide by the standard retail mark-up to get your wholesale price. If you aim to sell a dress at a retail price of $270, and divide by what is a fairly standard retail mark-up of 2.7 for designer boutiques, you get a wholesale price of $100. If you then decide to work to a 2.5 mark-up from cost price to wholesale price you can work out that you need to produce the dress for a cost price of $40.

The Cost of Goods spreadsheet can help here. If the dress is costing $45 to produce you can see which components are costing too much and which design elements you will have to change. If you decide to reduce your mark-up be sure that your business can handle the loss of income.

Alternatively, if the dress is costing only $36 to produce, your mark-up to wholesale will be closer to 2.8 and your profit margin greater.

Always ask buyers what mark-up they use to get their retail price. It is often a good idea to implement a manufacturer's suggested retail price (MSRP) to make sure your product is sold everywhere at the same price.

Mark-ups and Margins

Mark-up and margin are different ways of calculating profit, and the difference can be confusing. The mark-up is the percentage of the cost price you add to get the selling price. A 150 percent mark-up on a product that has cost you $50 would mean a selling price of $125. This is often also expressed as a mark-up of 2.5 (125 ÷ 50 = 2.5).

A margin is the percentage of the final selling price that is profit. If you are selling a product at $150 that cost you $50 to make, your margin would be 66 percent ([150 – 50] ÷ 150 x 100 = 66 percent). Just remember that a selling price with a margin of 50 percent results in more profit than a selling price with a mark-up of 50 percent (see box opposite). For example, if a sweater is selling for $100 and is clearing a 50 percent margin, it cost $50. If the same sweater had a mark-up of 50 percent, the retail price would be $75, with $25 less profit.

Any profit you calculate in this way will be considered your *gross* profits. You will still need to deduct your overheads (rates, fixed costs, corporation tax, wages, etc.), also known as indirect costs, before you arrive at your net profit.

You may find it easier to be flexible and have a different mark-up for each product in your range. This will give you a variety of mark-ups in your product line. So, if you were selling men's and women's jeans, you might find that your women's range can tolerate a mark-up of only twice the cost (or 100 percent), but that your men's range market can tolerate a mark-up of 3.5 times cost (or 250 percent). Over time you will become better at reading the market value and at maximizing your overall profit margins.

Tips for Calculating Margins

==

You will often have to calculate margins, perhaps to work out a selling price from a cost price, or to work out what margin a certain selling price would result in.

Selling price from cost price
The full formula for working out a selling price from a cost price and a certain margin is:

Selling = cost ÷ ([100 – margin] ÷ 100)
So to work out the selling price of a pair of jeans with a 70% margin that cost $30 to make, the calculation would look like this: 30 ÷ ([100 – 70] ÷ 100) = $100.

Alternatively you can simplify the calculation by using the following:

25% margin = cost price ÷ 0.75
40% margin = cost price ÷ 0.6
50% margin = cost price ÷ 0.5
70% margin = cost price ÷ 0.3.

Margin from cost and selling prices
Sometimes you will have a cost and a selling price, and need to know what margin that results in. The formula is:

Margin = (1 – [cost ÷ selling]) x 100
So the calculation of the margin for jeans selling for $100 that cost $30 to make would look like this: (1 – [30 ÷ 100]) x 100 = 70%.

Or to simplify you can use the following:

If cost ÷ selling is 0.6, the margin is 40%
If cost ÷ selling is 0.5, the margin is 50%
If cost ÷ selling is 0.3, the margin is 70%
If cost ÷ selling is 0.25, the margin is 75%.

Gross profit
Gross profit is the difference between your sales income and the cost of making your product.

Gross profit = selling price – direct costs

If direct cost = $50 and I mark it up 2.2 I will get a selling price of $110 and my gross profit will be $60. If I then sell 1,000 pieces at $110, I will make $110,000 worth of sales. However, if I subtract my original cost of $50 per garment (1,000 x $50 = $50,000) then my gross profit will be $60,000.

Net profit
Net profit is the money left after subtracting all your indirect costs away from your gross profit.

Net profit = gross profit – indirect costs

If my indirect costs for example were $55,000 then my net profit from the $60,000 gross would be $5,000. Net profit is the money you could pump back into your business.

==

Keeping the Books

While a business may be able to sustain itself for a short period without sales or profits, without cash it can't function. You must keep a close eye on your financial accounts and monitor your inflow and outflow of cash.

In order to make a profit, you will often have to deliver goods to your customers before payments are received. If you don't have enough money at your disposal to pay your suppliers and staff before your stockists pay you, you'll be unable to deliver your goods and make a profit.

To trade effectively and grow your business, you will need to build up cash reserves by ensuring that the timing of cash movements in and out of your account puts you in an overall positive cash flow situation.

Cash Flow

==

Cash is the measure of your ability to pay your bills on a regular basis.

Your cash includes: *Coins and notes, current accounts and short-term deposits, bank overdrafts and short-term loans, foreign currency and deposits that can be quickly converted to your currency.*

Your cash does not include: *Long-term deposits, long-term borrowing, accounts receivable from customers and inventory.*

==

Cash Flow Forecasting

The cash flow forecast will typically look at the upcoming quarter or year by month and will show both the cash coming into your business, and from where, as well as the cash going out and where it will go. It will focus on receipts, payments, excess of receipts over payments—with negative figures shown in brackets, opening bank balance, closing bank balance. It is important to be realistic about your potential sales growth for the next year. One way of doing this is to take your sales revenues for the previous 12-month period and add on the percentage predicted for the next year's economic growth.

Book-keeping

By law you must keep financial records and hold on to them for a seven-year period. The records you keep will need to be accurate and regularly updated, as you will have to pay a financial penalty if you cannot prove the information you have submitted on your Federal and State income tax returns. The two most important records you need to keep will be:

1   Receipts and expenditure of the business

2   Purchase and cost of goods sold.

Tips for Effective Book-keeping

What you need to do	When (minimum timescale recommended)
Record sales in the sales ledger	Contemporaneously
Record payments received in the sales ledger	Contemporaneously
Record purchases in the purchase ledger	Contemporaneously
Record payments made in the purchase ledger	Contemporaneously
Reconcile the sales and purchase ledgers	Every month
Pursue all outstanding payments	As soon as they are overdue
Reconcile your cash accounts against your bank statements and your sales and purchase ledgers against your cash accounts	Every month

These days most new business owners keep their records on computer but paper records are just as valid. What's important is that they are accurate and up-to-date. If you feel that this is an area that you might struggle with, there are a number of options available to you:

1   There are software packages that will provide a framework for keeping your accounts. When you set up your business bank account you may be offered one of these. However, you might end up spending money on a product that you still don't quite understand and are unable to use. Two of the most used on the market are QuickBooks and SAGE. The internet and your accountant can offer a good overview of assessing your business needs for an accounting package.

2   Your accountant will probably offer a book-keeping service. The better the state of the records you hand over, the less time it will take to do the books and the more money you will save. Your accountant will have software for record-keeping, so don't spend out on a software package if you don't need one.

3   Independent book-keepers. You may want to find an independent local book-keeper able to come to your office once every two weeks or once a month, depending on your needs. Check local directories and online for book-keepers advertising their services, or ask for a referral from your accountant or another local business.

4   Many government-funded small business support organizations offer free financial record-keeping set-up services whereby they come to your premises and set up a basic book-keeping spreadsheet, giving you a brief tutorial on what information needs to be input and when. Check online to see what is available to you.

Sales Tax

If you will have any retail or internet sales or will sell your samples after your season, you will be required to file quarterly sales tax returns. The amount of sales tax charged is determined locally in the community in which your business is located or the county to which you ship your goods. Many states and localities require the filing of quarterly or annual sales tax returns even if you will have no retail sales. Check with your local or state taxing authorities or your accountant when you form your business entity.

Improving Everyday Cash Flow

For any small business cash flow can be tricky, but within the fashion industry (and especially if you are working to the two-season-a-year wholesale calendar) it can be doubly so. There are a few things you can do to try to make life easier for yourself. (And see Tips for Improving Your Cash Flow, overleaf.)

Ask customers to pay sooner

Most boutiques, independent stores, and department stores will expect credit and will pay you after the goods have been received. This means you could be looking at only two windows a year when money will be coming into the business. To avoid this, ask for a deposit on confirmation of the order. This is usually to cover the costs of production and can cover you in case the store goes out of business or reneges on the order mid-season. It is also worth asking for the remainder of the payment pro forma when the goods are ready to be delivered. This means the store pays you as soon as the goods are with you and ready to go—once the monies have cleared, the goods are shipped. Even if the store won't pay the full amount pro forma it may be worth trying to negotiate 50 percent of the outstanding balance pro forma and giving credit (30 days is standard) for the remainder.

Use a factor

When you have sent your delivery to your stockists you send your invoices for each customer to a factor, who typically advances up to 80 or 90 percent of the invoice amount to you. The final balance is paid to you, minus the factor's fees, when your customer makes payment directly to the factor. Your customer will receive a letter from your factor with your invoice, and payment instructions. It can take as little as 24 hours for the funds to be released to you.

The factor's fees are calculated as a service charge of 0.6–3.0 percent of the invoiced amount, and interest charge on the cash advances. The service charge will be based on your annual turnover, number of invoices, and number of customers. The interest charge is typically comparable to normal secured bank overdraft rates.

Factors will offer a range of services. Typically the most common are: recourse factoring, when the risk of bad debts remains with you; and non-recourse factoring, when the factor protects you when customers fail to pay. With non-recourse factoring the factor typically covers the risk by taking out credit insurance. The cost of the credit insurance will then be passed on to you at around 0.3–0.7 percent of sales, depending on the risk profile of your customers and the amount you factor. It is common now for most factors to offer you the facility of monitoring your account online.

You will find a list of factors on the International Factoring Association website (*www.factoring.org*).

Ask for extended credit terms with suppliers
Most businesses are looking to develop long-term relationships with their customers, which means there may be room to ask for extended credit from your suppliers. This usually means setting up an account, but a 30-day grace period before payment is due can make a huge difference to your cash flow.

Negotiate a split delivery
With certain suppliers it may be worth seeing if it is possible to arrange a split delivery of goods. You may have a group of customers requiring delivery of their spring/summer stock in mid-January while another group are more than happy to take delivery at the end of February. By negotiating a split delivery with your manufacturer you would first receive and pay for the goods needing to be sent out in January; 30 days later you would receive and pay for the remainder of the order.

Increasing borrowing, or putting more money into the business
You should consider this option only for dealing with short-term downturns in income or if you are looking to fund expansion of your business in line with your business plan. It should not form the foundation of your cash flow strategy.

A Bathing Ape works hard to develop and maintain its brand identity to gain the trust of its customers. Likewise, you will need to develop and maintain a trust between yourself and your suppliers in order to obtain the most favorable payment terms

Tips for Improving Your Cash Flow

==

✖ *Issue invoices promptly and regularly chase outstanding payments.*

✖ *Consider exercising your right to charge penalty interest for late payment.*

✖ *Consider offering discounts for prompt payment (it's not uncommon for big department stores to tell you that they will take a percentage off the invoice for paying on time).*

✖ *Ask for a credit reference from other fashion labels that supply a new customer you are selling to, to see what kind of payers they are and therefore what terms you should offer.*

✖ *Make sure you deliver on time, to specification, and with good quality to avoid any late or lost revenue.*

✖ *Target new customers efficiently to maximize income and minimize expenses.*

✖ *Make sure your suppliers are not overcharging and are delivering on time with good quality.*

==

Quite often the key to good cash flow for a small fashion business is to be as creative with your financial structures as you are with your design and marketing. Constantly monitor the situation in the same way as for new trends on the catwalk or Rodeo Drive. Look for opportunities to save money and negotiate where possible.

Jay R. Horowitz CPA

Cost of Goods Spreadsheet

Season:		Style Number:	
		Style Name:	

Piece Goods	Description	Cost Per Meter	Meterage Required	Cost
Fabric 1				
Fabric 2				
Fabric 3				
Lining				
Interfacing				
Other				
Allowance				
			Subtotal	

Trimmings	Description	Unit Cost	Number of Units	Cost
Buttons				
Zippers				
Threads				
Labels				
Trims 1				
Trims 2				
			Subtotal	

Labor		Cost
Machinist		
Pattern cutting		
Grading		
Sewing		
	Subtotal	

Shipping		Cost
Bags/boxes		
Hangers		
Swing tickets		
Other		
	Subtotal	

Total Cost of Goods Sold	
Wholesale Mark-up	
Wholesale Price	
Retail Mark-up	
MSRP	

Case Study: Caroline Charles

Caroline Charles has been one of the UK's leading womenswear fashion designers since setting up her label in the 1960s. Over the past 40 years she has established the Caroline Charles brand throughout the world by offering modern, easy, useful, lasting, and ageless designs to an international client list of women with a hectic working, travel, and social life. Throughout an illustrious career that has seen her dress pop stars, movie stars, and royalty, Caroline has been at the forefront of the British fashion industry, receiving, in her fortieth year of operation, an OBE for services to the fashion industry.

She says, "The right time to start retailing is when you feel the customers will follow," and that to deliver a successful product you should offer "design for the customers' needs and tempt them with extras—think in terms of color groups, occasions, travel, weather, etc."

Caroline's vision and creative approach have remained steadfast since the conception of the label. She has a true belief in the style that she represents and is a perfectionist in every detail of the production, display, and selling of the products. Admitting to being "tremendously driven," she is hands-on in every aspect of her business, and is quick to point out she has the backing of "the best team in London."

Caroline designs three collections each season, all of which show off her love of textiles, cut, and finish. Her Caroline Charles London line is dedicated to celebrations, parties, and performances. The Caroline Collection moves the focus to jeans, suede leather, embroidery, T-shirts, knitwear, skirts, and shirts, while the Caroline Charles Studio line offers a limited edition collection focusing on eveningwear made in luxurious fabrics, many of which have been embroidered and beaded by hand.

Each range offers the Caroline Charles customer something different and Caroline works hard to maintain the brand's identity and USPs by focusing on specialized fabrics, textures, weaves, embroidery, beading, and novelties.

Although stocked in leading boutiques and department stores around the world, Caroline is a keen advocate of retailing her own product: "In your own retail space you are able to decorate/merchandise your clothes to their best advantage, while with wholesaling you rely on others to express their taste." Caroline opened her first retail store in the 1970s on Beauchamp Place, Knightsbridge, in the heart of London, and since then has used a successful retail strategy to develop her business.

Caroline has opened stores in a number of locations but has always tried to "get a shop with the highest footfall/passing trade that budget will allow," and says it is important to "be as close to similarly priced products as possible." She has negotiated a number of leases for her retail premises and believes that the best are 25-year leases, with breakpoints after one, two, and five years. "The breakpoints give the opportunity to take your business elsewhere if the location is not working." Sometimes negotiating "a turnover rent can also work well, i.e. pay the landlord 10 percent of the annual turnover for two years, then negotiate a fixed sum based on those figures."

Caroline sees getting the right staff to run her stores as being as important as the product. "Employ people who enjoy selling and who are very friendly and helpful. Natural shopkeepers love dressing the shop and moving the product around each week, including window-dressing." She also says it is important that terms and conditions for customer service and staff should be clearly thought-out. Within this she includes dress codes for staff—they play an important role in determining the brand image and therefore need to look the part.

Caroline believes it is important to set "sales targets against your budget and year on year make a percentage increase to those targets." However, she is not one to say no to a great find for a piece to sell in the shop and is quick to say, "Do not resist some irresistible accessory!"

One last essential ingredient for Caroline's retail success to date has been "good PR and a good mailing list." These, she says, are "essential to keep reminding people that you are open!"

Caroline Charles is one of the UK's top fashion designers and has built a successful business over the past 40 years, with a strong emphasis on her own retail outlets

Suggested Reading and Resources

Books

Color Forecasting for Fashion by Kate Scully and Debra Johnston Cobb (Laurence King Publishing, 2012)

An in-depth look into the color forecasting industry that will help you understand how colors behave and put together a palette for a successful collection.

Fashion Buying by Helen Goworek (Blackwell Publishing, second edition 2007)

This book describes the buying cycle, buying for stores and mail order, and how to start a career in fashion buying. A glossary of buying terminology, as well as input from fashion buyers currently working for major companies, gives a clear insight into this exciting and challenging role.

The Fashion Designer Survival Guide: Start and Run Your Own Fashion Business by Mary Gehlhar (Kaplan Trade, revised edition 2008)

Provides the necessary tools to get a fashion line or label up and moving on the right track.

Fashion Entrepreneur: Starting Your Own Fashion Business by Sandra Burke (Burke Publishing, 2008)

This book outlines the traits and techniques fashion designers use to set up small businesses. The topics include creativity and innovation, writing business plans, raising finance, sales and marketing, and the small-business management skills needed to run a creative company on a day-to-day basis.

Fashion Now: A Global Perspective by Celia Stall-Meadows (Prentice Hall, 2011)

A business-focused approach to the fashion industry, concentrating on identifying and meeting consumer demand. Includes a section on starting a fashion retail business.

Fashion Supply Chain Management: Industry and Business Analysis by Tsan-Ming Choi (IGI Global, 2012)

Helps you understand and control the supply chain, thus staying competitive.

Fashion & Sustainability: Design for Change by Kate Fletcher and Lynda Grose (Laurence King Publishing, 2012)

Looks at environmentally aware innovations throughout the fashion supply chain and examines how designers can work in more sustainable ways.

Footwear Design by Aki Choklat (Laurence King Publishing, 2012)

Illustrated guide to designing a footwear collection, including cutting-edge techniques.

Mastering Fashion Buying and Merchandising Management by Tim Jackson and David Shaw (Palgrave Macmillan, 2000)

Covers fashion design, merchandise planning, sources, and supply chain management.

Merchandising of Fashion Products by Doris H. Kincade and Fay Y. Gibson (Prentice Hall, 2010)

Guide to fashion merchandising from the initial concept to delivery in-store.

The Why of the Buy: Consumer Behavior and Fashion Marketing by Patricia M. Rath (Fairchild Books, 2008)

This book will help you understand why consumers buy what they do, and when, related to production and promotion in the fashion industry.

Websites

American Apparel & Footwear Association
www.wewear.org

Angel Capital Association
www.angelcapitalassociation.org

Angel Financing
www.angelfinancing.net

The Berg Fashion Library
www.bergfashionlibrary.com

Council of Fashion Designers of America
www.cfda.com

Counselors to America's Small Business
www.score.org

The Fashion Center
www.fashioncenter.com

Fashion Enter
www.fashion-enter.com

Fashion Incubator: Lessons from the Sustainable
Factory Floor
www.fashion-incubator.com

Fashion Industry Network
www.fashionindustrynetwork.com/

The Fashion Listings
www.thenationalregister.com

Fashion Schools
www.fashion-schools.org/

Bankrate (financing rates and sources)
www.bankrate.com

Government Grants
www.governmentgrants.org

Mercedes-Benz Fashion Week
www.mbfashionweek.com/

NPD Group (fashion market research)
*www.npd.com/wps/portal/npd/us/industryexpertise/
fashion*

Patent Office
www.uspto.gov

Small Business Administration
www.sba.gov

Tobe Group (fashion retail consultants)
www.tobereport.com/pages/

The Vogue Archive (every issue of the
magazine online)
www.vogue.com/archive

WeConnect Fashion
weconnectfashion.com/

Women's Wear Daily
www.wwd.com/

Directories

Men and Boys' Manufacturers Apparel Directory
(Marche Publishing, 9th edition 2011)

The National Register of the Apparel Marketplace
(Marche Publishing, 4th edition 2008)

*The National Register of Independent Sales Reps
(Apparel & Accessories)* (Marche Publishing, 7th
edition 2008)

Plunkett's Apparel & Textiles Industry Almanac 2009
by Jack W. Plunkett (Plunkett Research, 2009)

*Women and Children's Manufacturers Apparel
Directory* (Marche Publishing, 10th edition 2010)

Women's & Children's Wear Buyers, 2012–2013
(Salesman's Guide, 2012)

Glossary

agent—person authorized to act on your behalf in selling your product.

bespoke—individually or custom made.

block—primary pattern used time and again allowing designers to modify key silhouettes.

boutique—small shopping outlet specializing in elite and fashionable items.

buyer—person responsible for purchasing your product from you in order to sell on to the consumer.

C&F—Cost and Freight, a trading term to denote that the price of goods includes the main freight to a named port of destination.

call sheet—list of contact details of all the team members working on a shoot or catwalk show.

cash flow—measure of a company's financial health.

cash flow forecast—an estimate of a company's inflows and outflows of money measured over a specific period of time.

catwalk—where models parade the latest collections.

chain store—one of a number of retail stores under the same ownership and dealing in the same merchandise.

CIF—Cost, Insurance, and Freight paid to a point of destination and included in the price quoted.

CMT—manufacturing terminology for Cut, Make, Trim.

COD—Cash on Delivery. A transaction in which goods are paid for in full, in cash or by certified check, when they are delivered.

cognitive dissonance—anxiety resulting from inconsistency between one's beliefs and one's actions. Often occurs after the purchase of an expensive item.

comparative shopping—researching current products on the market offered by competitors.

cooperative—a business owned and controlled equally by the people who use its services or who work at it.

copyright—exclusive legal right to reproduce, publish, sell, or distribute artistic work.

cottage industry—business or industry in which goods are produced primarily in the home of the producer.

creative director—person responsible for developing and maintaining the overall image of the business.

cutting ticket—exact details for an order set for production, otherwise known as the production run.

department store—large retail store offering a variety of merchandise and services.

digital workflow—digital version of photographic film processing.

discount store—store that sells merchandise at a discount from the manufacturer's suggested retail price.

distribution—supply and delivery of fashion goods to warehouses, stores, and other outlets.

docket—see cutting ticket.

domain name—name that identifies a website.

e-commerce—buying and selling via the internet.

eco fashion—fashion designed to be environmentally friendly.

editorial shoot—photographic spread or spreads that tell a story and create an atmosphere.

employers' liability insurance—compulsory insurance policy for employers, protecting employees if they are injured or become ill as a result of their work.

entrepreneur—person that starts a new business venture.

equity stake—the proportion of a business owned by shareholders.

exchange of letters—an agreement or understanding between two parties.

exclusivity—one party grants another party sole rights with regard to a particular business function.

ex-factory—shipping term meaning that the seller owns goods until they are picked up from his factory, at which point they are the buyer's responsibility.

factor—third party who provides the seller with cash by purchasing, or taking a lien against, the accounts receivable or inventories of the seller.

fashion cupboard—where fashion magazines organize/store garments called in for photographing.

fast fashion—quick manufacturing at lower prices for the retail chains, in response to designer trends as they emerge.

fit model—model with standard proportions who tries on samples to get fit right.

FOB—Free On Board. A shipping term indicating that the supplier pays the shipping costs (and usually also the insurance costs) from the point of manufacture to a specified destination, at which point the buyer takes responsibility.

font—a specific typeface in a specific point size and style.

franchise—right to market a product or provide a service as granted by a manufacturer or company.

full package manufacturing—when a manufacturer provides all elements including patterns, fabric, cut, make, and all trims.

gross profit—profit before overheads (fixed operating expenses) have been deducted.

haute couture—clothes made exclusively for private clients.

high end—expensive designs below haute couture level, often produced in limited numbers.

indirect cost—cost not directly attributable to the manufacturing of a product, also known as overhead.

invoice—bill issued by the provider of products and/or services to a customer.

landed price—the total cost of a landed shipment including purchase price, freight, insurance, and other costs up to the port of destination. In some instances, it may include customs duties and other taxes levied on the shipment.

LDP—Landed Duty Paid, the price of goods including insurance, freight, and all duties.

lead time—time taken for supplier to make goods available.

letter of credit—document issued by a bank on the instruction of a buyer, authorizing a seller to draw a sum of money under specified terms, usually the receipt by the bank of certain documents within a given time.

licensing—permission to use intellectual property rights, such as trademarks, patents, or technology, under defined conditions.

line sheet—selling tool showing sketches of product with pricing, color options, and sizes.

logo—name, symbol, or trademark designed for easy and definite recognition.

lookbook—marketing tool showing photographs of a collection.

made-to-measure—garment fitted to the customer's size.

margin—net sales minus the cost of goods and services sold.

mark-up—amount added to a cost price in calculating selling price.

mass-market fashion—ready-to-wear clothes produced in large quantities and standard sizes using cheaper materials.

minimums—smallest amount of goods a seller will allow a buyer to purchase.

model release form—contract establishing the permitted use of a model's image.

mood board—sketches, colors, images, ideas used as the starting point for designs and collections.

motif—sewn or printed decoration synonymous with a brand.

MSRP—Manufacturer's Suggested Retail Price.

net profit—how much money a company has earned from its business over the course of a year.

net sales—sales generated by a company after the deduction of returns, allowances for damaged or missing goods, and any discounts allowed.

net terms—period of credit before payment is due.

offer—a designer's product range.

overhead—ongoing administrative expense of a business, not attributed to any specific business activity, but still necessary for the business to function; also known as indirect cost.

PDS—Pattern Design System, used to electronically cut and grade patterns.

perceived value—market-based approach to pricing, where the price is set by estimating potential consumers' perceptions of the value of the product.

pre-collection—delivered months ahead of a designer's main catwalk ranges, a preview of the new season's looks.

press book—folder for press cuttings.

press pack—collection of public relations material for distribution to the press.

press release—announcement of an event, performance, or other newsworthy item issued to the press.

prêt-à-porter—ready-to-wear clothing.

price architecture—framework in which a product is costed.

price point—standard price set by the seller for a product.

product portfolio—set of different products a fashion label produces.

pro forma—invoice presented for payment of goods prior to their dispatch.

range depth—the number of styles offered in a range.

range width—the number of color options for each style.

ranges—styles and collections.

range plan—detailed structure of a designer's collection prior to development of samples.

retail—sale of goods directly to the consumer.

ready-to-wear—clothing marketed in a finished condition, in standard clothing sizes.

runway—another term for catwalk.

samples—first versions of a design.

seasons—fall/winter and spring/summer styles and collections.

sell-through rate—percentage of stock sold prior to mark-downs.

shelf-life—time a product can be kept in store.

show card—card-mounted press clipping.

sourcing—researching, finding, and obtaining materials, trimmings, and finished garments.

specification drawing/spec—technical drawing showing all measurements of a product.

specification sheet—document including specification drawing, listing all the relevant components needed to make up a first sample.

specialty store—store selling only one type of merchandise.

split delivery—order delivered in more than one batch.

story—mood and direction of your collection.

story board—summary of your collection's inspiration and theme.

supply chain—system of organizing people, activities, information, and resources to get product from manufacturer to customer.

swatch—small piece of fabric used to illustrate color, print, design, or detail before a piece is made or delivered.

swing ticket—tag put on products showing price, size, and designer's logo/motif.

tear sheet—page cut or torn from a magazine, newspaper, or journal.

termination clause—provision in a contract that allows for its termination under specified circumstances.

territory—a specified geographical area or market.

toile—first made-up version of a garment in a cheap fabric.

trial balloon—a test of public opinion.

turnover—total sales made in a given period of time.

unit price—cost or price of an item.

USP—Unique Selling Point.

wholesale—selling product to a retailer who sells on at a higher price.

working capital—cash available for day-to-day operations.

Index

Picture Credits

Page 6 © Peter Donaldson/Alamy / Page 8 © Paul Cunningham/Corbis / Page 11 Daniel Garrett for the British Fashion Council / Page 13 Photography Jessica Bonham, stylist Carley Hague, clothes Goodone AW11 / Page 14 Burton Retail Group / Page 16 Derek Henderson / Pages 21, 22 Noir / Pages 30–31 Yasmin Kianfar AW11 main picture and below center, SS11 below left, SS12 below right. All photography by Christina Smith / Page 32 Gil Carvalho / Pages 36, 41 Knomo / Page 42 © Tim Graham/Alamy / Page 45 PSC Photography / Page 46 Knomo / Pages 48–49 Simon Walsh / Page 50 PSC Photography / Pages 54–55 Ed Hardy / Pages 56, 59 Three's Company (Creative Consultants) Ltd. / Page 62 Derek Henderson / Page 63 Belle & Bunty / Page 65 Photography top left Ulla Nyeman, bottom left Annie Bundfuss, top and bottom right Jo Paterson / Page 66 David Hardy / Page 68 PhotoAlto/ Sigrid Olsson/Getty Images / Page 69 Schumacher / Page 71 London College of Fashion / Page 73 Belle & Bunty / Pages 76–77 Gil Carvalho / Page 78 Photography from Pure London, at London Olympia www.purelondon.com / Page 81 Courtesy Magic International / Page 82 Noir / Page 84 top Knomo / Page 84 bottom Caroline Charles / Page 87 Anne Fontaine/Satoru Umetsu—Nacasa & Partners / Page 88 TrendStop in conjunction with picture sourcing agent Fashionriot.com / Page 91 Noir / Page 95 Harrods/www.Prshots.com / Page 97 Belle & Bunty / Page 99 Schumacher / Page 101 Harrods/ www.Prshots.com / Page 103 Knomo / Page 104 Caroline Charles / Page 106 Image courtesy of James Thompson / Pages 110–111 Courtesy Odel plc / Page 112 David Hardy / Page 116 Belle & Bunty / Pages 117, 119 Three's Company (Creative Consultants) Ltd. / Page 121 Gil Carvalho / Pages 124, 128–129 Sam Scott Hunter / Pages 130, 133 Courtesy Magic International / Page 134 © Jens Kalaene/dpa/Corbis / Page 135 Courtesy Magic International / Page 140 Paul Smith Ltd. / Page 145 Harrods/www.Prshots.com / Page 150 Ally Ward / Pages 152–153 Derek Henderson / Page 154 Malcolm Crews / Pages 157, 159 Three's Company (Creative Consultants) Ltd. / Page 165 Ken Towner/Evening/Rex Features / Page 168 Mizani / Page 169 Knomo / Page 172 Three's Company (Creative Consultants) Ltd. / Pages 174–175 All pictures by Soulland / Page 176 Image courtesy of James Thompson / Pages 192–193 Caroline Charles.

Acknowledgments

My special thanks go to:

My publisher Laurence King, in particular Helen Rochester for seeing the potential for the book and commissioning it and Anne Townley, Melissa Danny, Sophie Drysdale and Clare Double for their experience, patience and perseverance in seeing me through the first and second editions of this book respectively.

Howard Harrison, Benoit Rescue & Alastair Hops at Knomo, Caroline Charles, Gil Carvalho, Karen Walker, Dorethee Schumacher, Anne Fontaine, Peter Ingwersen at Noir, Christian Audigier at Ed Hardy, Yasmin Kianfar, Christoher Raeburn, Otara Gunewardene at Odel, Deborah Medhurst at no added sugar, and Silas Adler at Soulland for all agreeing to be case studies and sharing their invaluable experiences. Also Malcolm Crews, Rikard Osterlund, Simon Assirati, Caroline Mackay, Nzinga Russell, Niki Turner, Suzanna Crabb, Kat & Oz Aalam, Ravi Mattu, Richard Spalding, James Vanderzee, Claire Hamer and Ally Ward for their contributions and authoritative views.

David Hardy, Malcolm Crews, James Thompson, Christina Smith, Jaana Jätyri at Trendstop, Anna Millhouse, and Rebecca Munro at London College of Fashion, Rupert Shreeve, British Fashion Council and London Fashion Week, Marisa de Saracho at Magic International for their support with the visual content of the book.

My Belle & Bunty and Three's Company team including my business partners Alice Shreeve and Hannah Coniam for their constant support and inspiration, Lizzie Harper and Kate Le Versha for all their help and patience no matter what the task and Camille Boyd for her fantastic support in researching potential case studies.

I'd also like to thank Wendy Malem, Linda Roberts, Barbara Bell, the whole Centre for Fashion Enterprise and London College of Fashion short courses teams and Claire DeBraekeleer and the British Council for continuing to give me the opportunities to travel the world and meet with just some of the incredibly exciting design and entrepreneurial talent that exists out there.

Lastly I would like to give a big thank you to all my family and friends and especially my incredibly talented and supportive wife Alice and my daughters Mae and Darcey, to whom I continue to dedicate this book.